Birnbaum

Cancún
Cozumel & Isla Mujeres

A BIRNBAUM TRAVEL GUIDE

Alexandra Mayes Birnbaum
EDITORIAL CONSULTANT

Lois Spritzer
Executive Editor

Laura L. Brengelman
Managing Editor

Mary Callahan
Senior Editor

Patricia Canole
Gene Gold
Jill Kadetsky
Susan McClung
Beth Schlau
Associate Editors

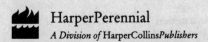

HarperPerennial
A Division of HarperCollinsPublishers

To Stephen, who merely made all this possible.

BIRNBAUM'S CANCUN, COZUMEL & ISLA MUJERES 94. Copyright © 1993 by HarperCollins Publishers. All rights reserved. Printed in the United States of America. No part of this book may be used or reproduced in any manner whatsoever without written permission except in the case of brief quotations embodied in critical articles and reviews. For information address HarperCollinsPublishers, 10 East 53rd Street, New York, NY 10022.

FIRST EDITION

ISSN 0749-2561 (Birnbaum Travel Guides)
ISSN 1055-5641 (Cancun, Cozumel & Isla Mujeres)
ISBN 0-06-278102-2 (pbk.)

93 94 95 96 97 CC/CW 10 9 8 7 6 5 4 3 2 1

Cover design © Drenttel Doyle Partners
Cover photograph © D&J Heaton/WestLight

BIRNBAUM TRAVEL GUIDES

Bahamas, and Turks & Caicos
Berlin
Bermuda
Boston
Canada
Cancun, Cozumel & Isla Mujeres
Caribbean
Chicago
Disneyland
Eastern Europe
Europe
Europe for Business Travelers
France
Germany
Great Britain
Hawaii
Ireland
Italy
London
Los Angeles
Mexico
Miami & Ft. Lauderdale
Montreal & Quebec City
New Orleans
New York
Paris
Portugal
Rome
San Francisco
Santa Fe & Taos
South America
Spain
United States
USA for Business Travelers
Walt Disney World
Walt Disney World for Kids, By Kids
Washington, DC

Contributing Editors
Frederick H. Brengelman
Wendy Luft
Thérèse Margolis
Carol Zaiser

Maps
B. Andrew Mudryk

Contents

Getting Ready to Go

Practical information for planning your trip.

Useful Words and Phrases

A collection of Spanish words and phrases to speed you
on your way. ... 33

The Islands

*A thorough, qualitative guide to Mexico's three most
often visited resort islands. This is a comprehensive
report on the most compelling attractions and
amenities — highlighting our top choices in every
category.*

Diversions

A selective guide to a variety of unexpected pleasures, pinpointing the best places in which to pursue them.

Directions

The Yucatán's major driving routes, leading from the country's most beautiful beaches to it's farthest jungles.

Foreword

My husband, Steve Birnbaum, and I never normally found ourselves particularly receptive to resorts designated by computer. Yet even I have to admit — however grudgingly — that the computer knew exactly what it was doing when it determined that Cancún, the ancient playground of the Maya, would make an equally appealing place in the sun for today's holidaymakers. If anything, Cancún — and the neighboring islands of Cozumel and Isla Mujeres — have suffered from the intense popularity spawned by the reliability of the local weather and the lure of wonderful sand beaches and irresistible Caribbean waters, so much so that there are those who now consider the region's national bird to be the construction crane.

Spectacular sand and sun notwithstanding, the last couple of years have been especially confusing for travelers heading for Mexico. The recent roller-coaster ride that has characterized Mexico's political, personal, financial, and industrial relationships with other North American countries — and the rest of the world, for that matter — has been mirrored by severe swings in currency relationships that have made an accurate estimation of the cost of a visit to Mexico very difficult. Clearly, there has never been a time when an up-to-date guide to Cancún, Cozumel, and Isla Mujeres was a more useful travel tool.

Obviously, any guidebook to Cancún and Cozumel must keep pace with and answer the real needs of today's travelers. That's why we've tried to create a guide that's specifically organized, written, and edited for the more demanding modern traveler, one for whom qualitative information is infinitely more desirable than mere quantities of unappraised data.

For years, dating back as far as Herr Baedeker, travel guides have tended to be encyclopedic, much more concerned with demonstrating expertise in geography and history than with a real analysis of the sorts of things that actually concern a typical modern tourist. I think you'll notice a different, more contemporary tone to our text, as well as an organization and focus that are distinctive and more functional. Early on, we realized that giving up the encyclopedic approach precluded our listing every single route and restaurant, a realization that helped define our overall editorial focus. Similarly, when we discussed the possibility of presenting certain information in other than strict geographic order, we found that the new format enabled us to arrange data in a way that best answers the questions travelers typically ask.

Travel guides are, understandably, reflections of personal taste, and putting one's name on a title page obviously puts one's preferences on the line. But I think I ought to amplify just what "personal" means. I don't believe in the sort of personal guidebook that's a palpable misrepresentation on its face. It is, for example, hardly possible for any single travel writer to visit thousands of restaurants (and nearly as many hotels) in any given year and provide accurate appraisals of each. And even if it were physically possible for one human being to survive such an itinerary, it would of necessity have to be done at a dead sprint, and the perceptions derived therefrom would probably be less valid than those of any other intelligent individual visiting the same establishments. It is, therefore, impossible (especially in a large, annually revised and updated guidebook *series* such as we offer) to have only one person provide all the data on the entire world.

I also happen to think that such individual orientation is of substantially less value to readers. Visiting a single hotel for just one night or eating one hasty meal in a random restaurant hardly equips anyone to provide appraisals that are of more than passing interest. We have, therefore, chosen what I like to describe as the "thee and me" approach to restaurant and hotel evaluation and, to a somewhat more limited degree, to the sites and sights we have included in our text. What this really reflects is personal sampling tempered by intelligent counsel from informed local sources, and these additional friends-of-the-editor are almost always residents of the island and/or area about which they are consulted.

In addition, very precise editing and tailoring keep our text fiercely subjective. So what follows is the gospel according to Birnbaum, and represents as much of our own taste and instincts as we can manage. It is probable, therefore, that if you like your beaches largely unpopulated, prefer small hotels with personality to huge high-rise anonymities, and can't tolerate fresh fish that's been relentlessly overcooked, we're likely to have a long and meaningful relationship.

I should also point out something about the person to whom this guidebook is directed. Above all, he or she is a "visitor." This means that such elements as restaurants have been specifically picked to provide the visitor with a representative, enlightening, stimulating, and above all pleasant experience. Since so many extraneous considerations can affect the reception and service accorded a regular restaurant patron, our choices can in no way be construed as an exhaustive guide to resident dining. We think we've listed all the best places, in various price ranges, but they were chosen with a visitor's enjoyment in mind.

Other evidence of how we've tried to tailor our text to reflect modern travel habits is most apparent in the section we call DIVERSIONS. Where once it was common for travelers to spend a visit to Mexico's resorts nailed to a single spot, seeing only the obvious sights, the emphasis today is more likely to be directed toward pursuing some special interest while seeing the surrounding countryside.

Therefore, we have collected these exceptional experiences so that it is no longer necessary to wade through a pound or two of superfluous prose just to find unexpected pleasures and treasures.

Although the sheer beauty of the Mexican Caribbean is reason enough to want to visit, there are also a number of added bonuses once you arrive. The entire adjacent Yucatán Peninsula offers a veritable cornucopia of activities to challenge the imagination of any visitor. Deep in the tropical jungles of the region lie archaeological treasures from one of the richest civilizations in human history. Naturalists also will find the region an ideal setting for studying flamingos, manatees, and even sharks in their natural habitats.

Finally, I also should point out that every good travel guide is a living enterprise; that is, no part of this text is carved in stone. In our annual revisions, we refine, expand, and further hone all our material to serve your travel needs better. To this end, no contribution is of greater value to us than your personal reaction to what we have written, as well as information reflecting your own experiences while using the book. Please write to us at 10 E. 53rd St., New York, NY 10022.

We sincerely hope to hear from you.

Alexandra Mayes Birnbaum

ALEXANDRA MAYES BIRNBAUM, editorial consultant to the *Birnbaum Travel Guides*, worked with her late husband Stephen Birnbaum as co-editor of the series. She has been a world traveler since childhood and is known for her lively travel reports on radio on what's hot and what's not.

Cancun

Cozumel & Isla Mujeres

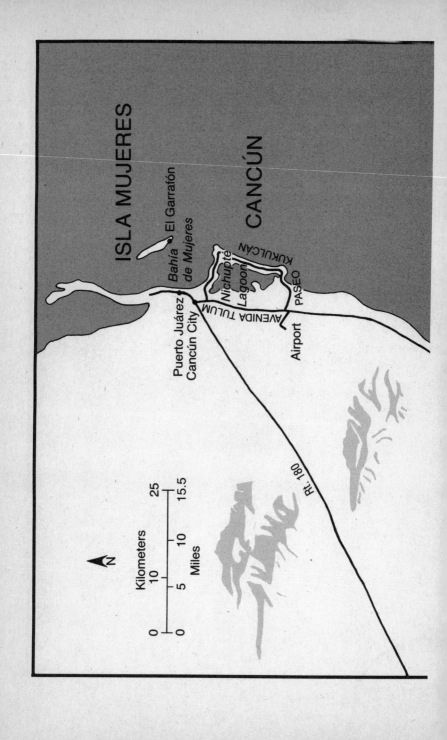

ISLA MUJERES

Bahía El Garrafón
de Mujeres

CANCÚN

Puerto Juárez
Cancún City

Nichupté
Lagoon

KUKULCÁN

PASEO

AVENIDA TULUM

Airport

Rt. 180

N

Kilometers
0   5   10   25
0   5   10   15.5
Miles

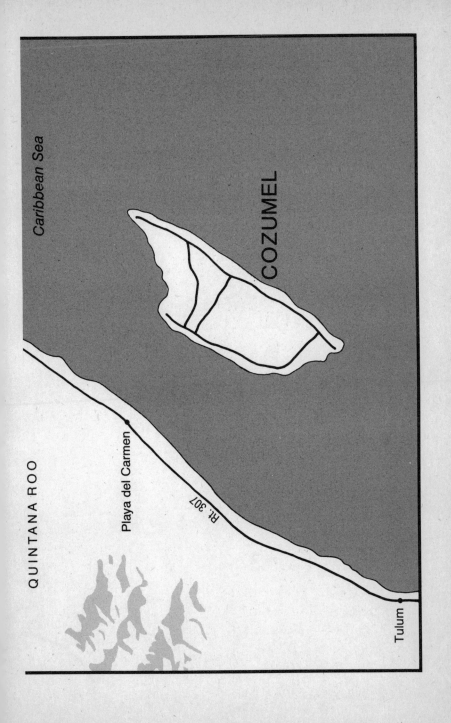

How to Use This Guide

A great deal of care has gone into the special organization of this guide-book, and we believe it represents a real breakthrough in the presentation of travel material.

Our text is divided into five basic sections in order to present information in the best way on every possible aspect of a vacation to Mexico's Caribbean Coast. Our aim is to highlight what's where and to provide basic information — how, when, where, how much, and what's best — to assist you in making the most intelligent choices possible.

Here is a brief summary of the five sections of this book, and what you can expect to find in each. We believe that you will find both your travel planning and on-island enjoyment enhanced by having this book at your side.

GETTING READY TO GO

A mini-encyclopedia of practical travel facts with all the precise data necessary to create a successful journey to and through Cancún, Cozumel, and Isla Mujeres, and along the Yucatán Peninsula. Here you will find how to get where you're going, plus selected resources — including useful publications, and companies and organizations specializing in discount and special-interest travel — providing a wealth of information and assistance useful both before and during your trip.

USEFUL WORDS AND PHRASES

Though most resorts in Cancún, Cozumel, and Isla Mujeres have English-speaking staff, at smaller establishments and on most stops along the Yucatán trail, a little knowledge of Spanish will go a long way. This collection of often-used words and phrases will help you to make a hotel or dinner reservation, order a meal, mail a letter — and even buy tooth-paste.

THE ISLANDS

Individual reports on Cancún, Cozumel, and Isla Mujeres offer a short-stay guide, including an essay introducing each island as a contemporary place to visit; *At-a-Glance* contains a site-by-site survey of the most important, interesting, and sometimes most eclectic sights to see and things to do; *Sources and Resources* is a concise listing of pertinent tourism information, such as the address of the local tourist office, which sightseeing tours to take, where to find the best nightspot, which shops have the finest merchandise and/or the most irresistible bargains, and where the best golf, tennis, fishing, and swimming are to be found. *Best in Town* lists our collection of cost-and-quality choices of the best places to eat and sleep on a variety of budgets.

DIVERSIONS

This section is designed to help travelers find the best places to engage in a variety of exceptional experiences for the mind and body, without having to wade through endless pages of unrelated text. In every case, our particular suggestions are intended to guide you to that special place where the quality of experience is likely to be highest.

DIRECTIONS

Here are four day trips from Cancún's superb beaches, plus two extended driving itineraries for exploring Maya relics on the Yucatán Peninsula. The itineraries can be connected for longer drives or used individually for short, intensive explorations.

Each entry includes a guide to sightseeing highlights; a qualitative guide to accommodations along the road (small inns, clean and comfortable motels, country hotels, campgrounds, and detours to off-the-main-road discoveries); hints and suggestions for activities; and detailed driving maps of the route, noting points of interest described in the text.

To use this book to full advantage, take a few minutes to read the table of contents and random entries in each section to get a firsthand feel for how it all fits together. You will find that the sections of this book are building blocks designed to help you put together the best possible trip. Use them selectively as a tool, a source of ideas, a reference work for accurate facts, and a guidebook to the best buys, the most exciting sights, the most pleasant accommodations, and the tastiest foods — *the best travel experience* that you can possibly have.

Getting
Ready to Go

When to Go

Cancún, Cozumel, and Isla Mujeres are blessed with year-round tourism seasons, so there really isn't a "best" time to visit. Winter is the most popular vacation time, but travel during the off-seasons (late spring, summer, and fall) and shoulder seasons (the months immediately before and after the peak months) also offers fair weather and smaller crowds. During these periods, travel also is less expensive.

The *Weather Channel* (2600 Cumberland Pkwy., Atlanta, GA 30339; phone: 404-434-6800) provides current weather forecasts. Call 900-WEATHER from any touch-tone phone in the US; the 95¢ per minute charge will appear on your phone bill.

Traveling by Plane

SCHEDULED FLIGHTS

Leading airlines offering flights between the US and Cancún include *Aeroméxico, American, Continental, Mexicana, Northwest,* and *United. Continental, Mexicana* and *Northwest* also offer flights to Cozumel.

FARES The great variety of airfares can be reduced to the following basic categories: first class, business class, coach (also called economy or tourist class), excursion or discount, and standby, as well as various promotional fares. For information on applicable fares and restrictions, contact the airlines listed above or ask your travel agent. Most airfares are offered for a limited time period. Once you've found the lowest fare for which you can qualify, purchase your ticket as soon as possible.

RESERVATIONS Reconfirmation is strongly recommended for all international flights. It is essential that you confirm your round-trip reservations — *especially the return leg* — as well as any flights within Mexico.

SEATING Airline seats usually are assigned on a first-come, first-served basis at check-in, although you may be able to reserve a seat when purchasing your ticket. Seating charts often are available from airlines and are included in the *Airline Seating Guide* (Carlson Publishing Co., PO Box 888, Los Alamitos, CA 90720; phone: 310-493-4877).

SMOKING US law prohibits smoking on flights scheduled for 6 hours or less within the US and its territories on both domestic and international carriers. These rules do not apply to nonstop flights between the US and international destinations. A free wallet-size guide that describes the rights of nonsmokers is available from *ASH* (*Action on Smoking and Health;* DOT Card, 2013 H St. NW, Washington, DC 20006; phone: 202-659-4310).

SPECIAL MEALS When making your reservation, you can request one of the airline's alternate menu choices for no additional charge. Call to reconfirm your request 24 hours before departure.

BAGGAGE On a major international airline, passengers usually are allowed to carry on board one bag that will fit under a seat or in an overhead bin. Passengers also can check two bags in the cargo hold, measuring 62 inches and 55 inches in combined dimensions (length, width, and depth) with a per-bag weight limit of 70 pounds. There may be charges for additional, oversize, or overweight luggage, and for special equipment or sporting gear. Note that baggage allowances may vary for children (depending on the percentage of full adult fare paid) and on domestic routes abroad. Check that the tags the airline attaches are correctly coded for your destination.

CHARTER FLIGHTS

By booking a block of seats on a specially arranged flight, charter operators frequently offer travelers bargain airfares. If you do fly on a charter, however, read the contract's fine print carefully. Charter operators can cancel a flight or assess surcharges of 10% of the airfare up to 10 days before departure. You usually must book in advance (no changes are permitted, so invest in trip cancellation insurance); also make your check out to the company's escrow account. For further information, consult the publication *Jax Fax* (397 Post Rd., Darien, CT 06820; phone: 203-655-8746).

DISCOUNTS ON SCHEDULED FLIGHTS

COURIER TRAVEL In return for arranging to accompany some kind of freight, a traveler may pay only a portion of the total airfare and a small registration fee. One agency that matches up would-be couriers with courier companies is *Now Voyager* (74 Varick St., Suite 307, New York, NY 10013; phone: 212-431-1616).

Courier Companies

Courier Travel Service (530 Central Ave., Cedarhurst, NY 11516; phone: 516-763-6898).

Discount Travel International (169 W. 81st St., New York, NY 10024; phone: 212-362-3636; and 940 10th St., Suite 2, Miami Beach, FL 33139; phone: 305-538-1616).

Excaliber International Courier (c/o *Way to Go Travel,* 6679 Sunset Blvd., Hollywood, CA 90028; phone: 213-466-1126).

F.B. On Board Courier Services (10225 Ryan Ave., Suite 103, Dorval, Quebec H9P 1A2, Canada; phone: 514-633-0740).

Halbart Express (147-05 176th St., Jamaica, NY 11434; phone: 718-656-8279).

International Adventures (60 E. 42nd St., New York, NY 10165; phone: 212-599-0577).

Midnight Express (925 W. High Park Blvd., Inglewood, CA 90302; phone: 310-672-1100).

Publications

Insider's Guide to Air Courier Bargains, by Kelly Monaghan (The Intrepid Traveler, PO Box 438, New York, NY 10034; phone: 212-304-2207).

Travel Secrets (PO Box 2325, New York, NY 10108, phone: 212-245-8703).

Travel Unlimited (PO Box 1058, Allston, MA 02134-1058; no phone).

World Courier News (PO Box 77471, San Francisco, CA 94107; no phone).

CONSOLIDATORS AND BUCKET SHOPS These companies buy blocks of tickets from airlines and sell them at a discount to travel agents or to consumers. Since many bucket shops operate on a thin margin, before parting with any money check the company's record with the Better Business Bureau.

Bargain Air (655 Deep Valley Dr., Suite 355, Rolling Hills, CA 90274; phone: 800-347-2345).

Council Charter (205 E. 42nd St., New York, NY 10017; phone: 800-800-8222 or 212-661-0311).

International Adventures (60 E. 42nd St., New York, NY 10165; phone: 212-599-0577).

Travac Tours and Charters (989 Ave. of the Americas, New York, NY 10018; phone: 800-872-8800 or 212-563-3303).

Unitravel (1177 N. Warson Rd., St. Louis, MO 63132; phone: 800-325-2222 or 314-569-0900).

LAST-MINUTE TRAVEL CLUBS For an annual fee, members receive information on imminent trips and other bargain travel opportunities. Despite the names of these clubs, you don't have to wait until literally the last minute to make travel plans.

Discount Travel International (114 Forest Ave., Suite 203, Narberth, PA 19072; phone: 215-668-7184).

Last Minute Travel (1249 Boylston St., Boston, MA 02215; phone: 800-LAST-MIN or 617-267-9800).

Moment's Notice (425 Madison Ave., New York, NY 10017; phone: 212-486-0500, -0501, -0502, or -0503).

Spur-of-the-Moment Cruises (411 N. Harbor Blvd., Suite 302, San Pedro, CA 90731; phone: 800-4-CRUISES in California; 800-343-1991 elsewhere in the US; or 310-521-1070).

> *Traveler's Advantage* (3033 S. Parker Rd., Suite 900, Aurora, CO 80014; phone: 800-548-1116 or 800-835-8747).
> *Vacations to Go* (1502 Augusta, Suite 415, Houston, TX 77057; phone: 713-974-2121 in Texas; 800-338-4962 elsewhere in the US).
> *Worldwide Discount Travel Club* (1674 Meridian Ave., Miami Beach, FL 33139; phone: 305-534-2082).

GENERIC AIR TRAVEL These organizations operate much like an ordinary airline standby service, except that they offer seats on not one but several scheduled and charter airlines. One pioneer of generic flights is *Airhitch* (2790 Broadway, Suite 100, New York, NY 10025; phone: 212-864-2000).

BARTERED TRAVEL SOURCES Barter is a common means of exchange between travel suppliers. Bartered travel clubs such as *Travel World Leisure Club* (225 W. 34th St., Suite 909, New York, NY 10122; phone: 800-444-TWLC or 212-239-4855) offer discounts to members for an annual fee.

CONSUMER PROTECTION

Passengers with complaints who are not satisfied with the airline's response can contact the US Department of Transportation (DOT; Consumer Affairs Division, 400 7th St. SW, Room 10405, Washington, DC 20590; phone: 202-366-2220). If you have a complaint against a local travel service, contact the Mexican tourist authorities. Also see *Fly Rights* (publication #050-000-00513-5; US Government Printing Office, PO Box 371954, Pittsburgh, PA 15250-7954; phone: 202-783-3238).

Traveling by Ship

Your cruise fare usually includes all meals, recreational activities, and entertainment. Shore excursions are available at extra cost, and can be booked in advance or once you're on board. An important factor in the price of a cruise is the location and size of your cabin; for information on ships' layouts and facilities, consult the charts issued by the *Cruise Lines International Association* (*CLIA;* 500 Fifth Ave., Suite 1407, New York, NY 10110; phone: 212-921-0066).

Most cruise ships have a doctor on board, plus medical facilities. The US Public Health Service (PHS) also inspects all passenger vessels calling at US ports; for the most recent summary or a particular inspection report, write to Chief, Vessel Sanitation Program, National Center for Environmental Health (1015 N. America Way, Room 107, Miami, FL 33132; phone: 305-536-4307). For further information, consult *Ocean and Cruise News* (PO Box 92, Stamford, CT 06904; phone: 203-329-2787). And for a free listing of travel agencies specializing in cruises, contact the *National Association of Cruise Only Agencies* (*NACOA;* PO Box 7209, Freeport, NY 11520; phone: 516-378-8006).

Cruise Lines

Carnival Cruise Lines (3655 NW 87th Ave., Miami, FL 33178-2428; phone: 800-327-9501).

Commodore Cruise Line (800 Douglas Rd., Suite 600, Coral Gables, FL 33134; phone: 800-237-5361, 800-327-5617, or 305-529-3000).

Crown Cruise Line (800 Douglas Rd., Suite 600, Coral Gables, FL 33134; phone: 800-237-5361 or 800-327-5617).

Cunard (555 Fifth Ave., New York, NY 10017; phone: 800-5-CUNARD or 800-221-4770).

Dolphin Cruise Line (901 S. America Way, Miami, FL 33132; phone: 800-222-1003).

Holland America Line (300 Elliot Ave. W., Seattle, WA 98119; phone: 800-426-0327).

Princess Cruises (10100 Santa Monica Blvd., Los Angeles, CA 90067; phone: 800-421-0522).

Regency Cruises (260 Madison Ave., New York, NY 10016; phone: 212-972-4774 in New York State; 800-388-5500 elsewhere in the US).

Royal Caribbean Cruise Lines (1050 Caribbean Way, Miami, FL 33132; phone: 800-432-6559 in Florida; 800-327-6700 elsewhere in the US).

Royal Viking Line (95 Merrick Way, Coral Gables, FL 33134; phone: 800-422-8000).

Sun Line (1 Rockefeller Plaza, Suite 315, New York, NY 10020; phone: 800-468-6400 or 212-397-6400).

Touring by Car

Driving is the most flexible way to explore Mexico on your way to or from Cancún. When planning your driving route, however, be *very* conservative in estimating driving time — *driving or stopping by the roadside after dark can be very dangerous.*

To drive in Mexico, a US citizen must have a valid US driver's license. Also required is a car permit, available from Mexican consulates in the US or from guards at the border for a $10 fee, which *must* be charged (to *American Express, MasterCard, or Visa*) or you will have to post a refundable bond from 10% to 100% of the car's value. Bring the car's registration and proof of ownership; if you are driving a car rented in the US or in a vehicle belonging to someone else, carry a notarized affidavit stating your right to drive the vehicle in Mexico.

You also must have proof of insurance coverage in the US, as well as separate Mexican insurance. Your insurance agent can have the policy written for you through a Mexican company, you can obtain coverage in any border town, or from *Sanborn's Mexico Insurance Service* (main office: 2009 S. 10th St., McAllen, TX 78502; phone: 512-686-0711). You'll also need *juridical insurance* — in case you damage federal property or injure a Mexican citizen while driving — from a company such as *Asociación*

Jurídica Automovilística (*AJA;* main office: 39 Montecito, Colonia Nápoles, México, DF 03810; phone: 5-687-3999). The Mexican government provides a toll-free number (phone: 800-446-8277) for information on car entry requirements.

MAPS

Among the best maps are those available from *Guía Roji* (31 J. Moran, México, DF 11850; phone: 5-702-0931). Others include those published by Mexico's *Dirección General de Geografía* (Mexico City sales office is at 71 Calle Balderas) and the *Servicio Meteorológico Nacional* (192 Av. Observatorio, Tacubaya, México, DF 11860). Also look for the *Rand McNally Cosmopolitan Map of Mexico* and the *Rand McNally Road Atlas: US, Canada and Mexico* (Rand McNally; 150 E. 52nd St., New York, NY 10022; phone: 212-758-7488). A good source for maps is *Map Link* (25 E. Mason St., Suite 201, Santa Barbara, CA 93101; phone: 805-965-4402).

AUTOMOBILE CLUBS AND BREAKDOWNS

To protect yourself in case of breakdowns while driving to and through Mexico, and for travel information and other benefits, consider joining a reputable automobile club. The largest of these is the *American Automobile Association* (*AAA;* 1000 AAA Dr., Heathrow, FL 32746-5063; phone: 407-444-8544). Before joining this or any other automobile club, check whether it has reciprocity with Mexican clubs such as *Asociación Mexicana Automovilística* (*AMA;* 7 Calle Orizaba, México, DF 06700; phone: 5-208-8329 or 5-511-6285) and the *Automóvil Club de México* (59 José Maria Iglesias, Colonia Tabacalera, Mexico City, México, DF 06030; phone: 5-705-0258).

Major Mexican highways are patrolled by the Mexican Secretary of Tourism's Green Angels *(Angeles Verdes)* fleet of emergency service trucks; except for parts and fuel, their assistance is free. Tourists also can call 915-250-8221. In Mexico, CB radio channels 9 and 11 are designated for travel emergencies.

GASOLINE

Pemex (an acronym for *Petróleos Mexicanos*) is the only brand sold in Mexico. Gasoline is sold in liters (about 3.7 liters to 1 gallon). Leaded (*Nova*), unleaded (*Magna sin*), and diesel fuel are available.

RENTING A CAR

You can rent a car through a travel agent or international rental firm before leaving home, or from a local company once in Mexico. Reserve in advance.

Most car rental companies require a credit card, although some will accept a substantial cash deposit. The minimum age to rent a car is set by the company; some impose special conditions on drivers above a certain age. Electing to pay for collision damage waiver (CDW) protection will add to the cost of renting a car, but releases you from financial liability for the vehicle. Additional costs include drop-off charges or one-way service fees.

International Car Rental Companies
Auto Europe (phone: 800-223-5555).
Avis (phone: 800-331-1084).
Budget (phone: 800-472-3325).
Dollar Rent A Car (phone: 800 800-4000).
Hertz (phone: 800-654-3001).
National (phone: 800-227-3876).

National Car Rental Companies
Alpri Rent a Car (phone: 5-564-2543 or 5-564-5076 for the main office in Mexico City).
Economovil Rent (phone: 5-604-5960 or 5-604-2118 for the main office in Mexico City).
Rentacar Monroy (phone: 5-564-7182 for the main office in Mexico City).

Package Tours

A package is a collection of travel services that can be purchased in a single transaction. Its principal advantages are convenience and economy — the cost is usually lower than that of the same services bought separately. Tour programs generally can be divided into two categories: escorted or locally hosted (with a set itinerary) and independent (usually more flexible).

When considering a package tour, read the brochure *carefully* to determine what is included and other conditions. Check the company's record with the Better Business Bureau. The *United States Tour Operators Association* (*USTOA;* 211 E. 51st St., Suite 12B, New York, NY 10022; phone: 212-944-5727) also can be helpful in determining a package tour operator's reliability. As with charter flights, always make your check out to the company's escrow account.

Many tour operators offer packages focused on special interests such as nature study, sports, and other recreations. *All Adventure Travel* (PO Box 4307, Boulder, CO 80306; phone: 800-537-4025 or 303-499-1981) represents such specialized packagers; some also are listed in the *Specialty Travel Index* (305 San Anselmo Ave., Suite 313, San Anselmo, CA 94960; phone: 415-459-4900 in California; 800-442-4922 elsewhere in the US).

Package Tour Operators
Adventure Center (1311 63rd St., Suite 200, Emeryville, CA 94608; phone: 510-654-1879 in northern California; 800-227-8747 elsewhere in the US).

Adventure Tours (9819 Liberty Rd., Randallstown, MD 21133; phone: 410-922-7000 in Baltimore; 800-638-9040 elsewhere in the US).

American Express Vacations (offices throughout the US; phone: 800-241-1700 or 404-368-5100).

Apple Vacations East (7 Campus Blvd., Newtown Sq., PA 19073; phone: 800-727-3400).

Backroads (1516 5th St., Berkeley, CA 94710-1713; phone: 800-245-3874, 800-462-2848, or 510-527-1555).

Continental Grand Destinations (phone: 800-634-5555).

Delta's Dream Vacations (phone: 800-872-7786).

Far Horizons (PO Box 91900, Albuquerque, NM 87199-1900; phone: 800-552-4575).

Fishing International (PO Box 2132, Santa Rosa, CA 95405; phone: 800-950-4242 or 707-539-3366).

Frontiers International (PO Box 959, 100 Logan Rd., Wexford, PA 15090; phone: 412-935-1577 in Pennsylvania; 800-245-1950 elsewhere in the US).

Funway Holidays Funjet (PO Box 1460, Milwaukee, WI 53201-1460; phone: 800-558-3050).

GoGo Tours (69 Spring St., Ramsey, NJ 07446-0507; phone: 201-934-3500).

Maya Route Tours (PO Box 1948, Murray Hill Station, New York, NY 10156; phone: 212-683-2136 or 212-532-8370).

Mountain Travel-Sobek (6420 Fairmount Ave., El Cerrito, CA 94530; phone: 510-527-8100 in California; 800-227-2384 elsewhere in the US).

Northwest World Vacations (5130 Hwy. 101, Minnetonka, MN 55345; phone: 800-727-1111).

Outback Expeditions (PO Box 16343, Seattle, WA 98116; phone: 206-932-7012).

Plus Ultra Tours (174 7th Ave., New York, NY 10011; phone: 212-242-0393 in New York State; 800-242-0394 elsewhere in the US).

Questers Tours & Travel (257 Park Ave. S., New York, NY 10010; phone: 800-468-8668 or 212-673-3120).

Sanborn Tours (1007 Main St., Bastrop, TX 78602; phone: 800-531-5440 or 512-321-1131).

Trans National Travel (2 Charlesgate W., Boston, MA 02215; phone: 800-262-0123).

Trek America (PO Box 470, Blairstown, NJ 07825; phone: 800-221-0596 or 908-362-9198).

Wildland Adventures (3516 NE 155th St., Seattle, WA 98155; phone: 800-345-4453 or 206-365-0686).

Insurance

The first person with whom you should discuss travel insurance is your own insurance broker. You may discover that the insurance you already carry protects you adequately while traveling and that you need little additional coverage. If you charge travel services, the credit card company also may provide some insurance coverage (and other safeguards).

Types of Travel Insurance

Baggage and personal effects insurance: Protects your bags and their contents in case of damage or theft anytime during your travels.

Personal accident and sickness insurance: Covers cases of illness, injury, or death in an accident while traveling.

Trip cancellation and interruption insurance: Guarantees a refund if you must cancel a trip; may reimburse you for the extra travel costs incurred for catching up with a tour or traveling home early.

Default and/or bankruptcy insurance: Provides coverage in the event of default and/or bankruptcy on the part of the tour operator, airline, or other travel supplier.

Flight insurance: Covers accidental injury or death while flying.

Automobile insurance: Provides collision, theft, property damage, and personal liability protection while driving your own or a rented car.

Combination policies: Include any or all of the above.

Disabled Travelers

Make travel arrangements well in advance. Specify to all services involved the nature of your disability to determine if there are accommodations and facilities that meet your needs.

Organizations

ACCENT on Living (PO Box 700, Bloomington, IL 61702; phone: 309-378-2961).

Access: The Foundation for Accessibility by the Disabled (PO Box 356, Malverne, NY 11565; phone: 516-887-5798).

American Foundation for the Blind (15 W. 16th St., New York, NY 10011; phone: 800-232-5463 or 212-620-2147).

Information Center for Individuals with Disabilities (Ft. Point Pl., 1st Floor, 27-43 Wormwood St., Boston, MA 02210; phone: 800-462-5015 in Massachusetts; 617-727-5540 or 617-727-5541 elsewhere in the US; TDD: 617-345-9743).

Mobility International USA (*MIUSA;* PO Box 3551, Eugene, OR 97403; phone: 503-343-1284, both voice and TDD; main office: 228 Borough High St., London SE1 1JX, England; phone: 44-71-403-5688).

National Rehabilitation Information Center (8455 Colesville Rd., Suite 935, Silver Spring, MD 20910; phone: 301-588-9284).

Paralyzed Veterans of America (*PVA;* PVA/ATTS Program, 801 18th St. NW, Washington, DC 20006; phone: 202-872-1300 in Washington, DC; 800-424-8200 elsewhere in the US).

Partners of the Americas (1424 K St. NW, Suite 700, Washington, DC 20005; phone: 800-322-7844 or 202-628-3300).

Royal Association for Disability and Rehabilitation (*RADAR;* 25 Mortimer St., London W1N 8AB, England; phone: 44-71-637-5400).

Society for the Advancement of Travel for the Handicapped (*SATH;* 347 Fifth Ave., Suite 610, New York, NY 10016; phone: 212-447-7284).

Travel Information Service (MossRehab Hospital, 1200 W. Tabor Rd., Philadelphia, PA 19141-3099; phone: 215-456-9600; TDD: 215-456-9602).

Publications

Access Travel: A Guide to the Accessibility of Airport Terminals (Consumer Information Center, Dept. 578Z, Pueblo, CO 81009; phone: 719-948-3334).

Air Transportation of Handicapped Persons (publication #AC-120-32; US Department of Transportation, Distribution Unit, Publications Section, M-443-2, 400 7th St. SW, Washington, DC 20590).

The Diabetic Traveler (PO Box 8223 RW, Stamford, CT 06905; phone: 203-327-5832).

Directory of Travel Agencies for the Disabled and *Travel for the Disabled,* both by Helen Hecker (Twin Peaks Press, PO Box 129, Vancouver, WA 98666; phone: 800-637-CALM or 206-694-2462).

Guide to Traveling with Arthritis (Upjohn Company, PO Box 989, Dearborn, MI 48121).

The Handicapped Driver's Mobility Guide (*American Automobile Association,* 1000 AAA Dr., Heathrow, FL 32746; phone: 407-444-7000).

Handicapped Travel Newsletter (PO Box 269, Athens, TX 75751; phone: 903-677-1260).

Handi-Travel: A Resource Book for Disabled and Elderly Travellers, by Cinnie Noble (*Canadian Rehabilitation Council for the Disabled,* 45 Sheppard Ave. E., Suite 801, Toronto, Ontario M2N 5W9, Canada; phone: 416-250-7490, both voice and TDD).

Incapacitated Passengers Air Travel Guide (*International Air Transport Association,* Publications Sales Department, 2000 Peel St., Montreal, Quebec H3A 2R4, Canada; phone: 514-844-6311).

Ticket to Safe Travel (*American Diabetes Association,* 1660 Duke St., Alexandria, VA 22314; phone: 800-232-3472 or 703-549-1500).

Travel for the Patient with Chronic Obstructive Pulmonary Disease (Dr. Harold Silver, 1601 18th St. NW, Washington, DC 20009; phone: 202-667-0134).

Travel Tips for Hearing-Impaired People (*American Academy of Otolaryngology*, 1 Prince St., Alexandria, VA 22314; phone: 703-836-4444).

Travel Tips for People with Arthritis (*Arthritis Foundation*, 1314 Spring St. NW, Atlanta, GA 30309; phone: 800-283-7800 or 404-872-7100).

Traveling Like Everybody Else: A Practical Guide for Disabled Travelers, by Jacqueline Freedman and Susan Gersten (Modan Publishing, PO Box 1202, Bellmore, NY 11710; phone: 516-679-1380).

The Wheelchair Traveler, by Douglass R. Annand (123 Ball Hill Rd., Milford, NH 03055; phone: 603-673-4539).

Package Tour Operators

Accessible Journeys (35 W. Sellers Ave., Ridley Park, PA 19078; phone: 215-521-0339).

Accessible Tours/Directions Unlimited (Lois Bonnani, 720 N. Bedford Rd., Bedford Hills, NY 10507; phone: 800-533-5343 or 914-241-1700).

Beehive Business and Leisure Travel (1130 W. Center St., N. Salt Lake, UT 84054; phone: 800-777-5727 or 801-292-4445).

Classic Travel Service (8 W. 40th St., New York, NY 10018; phone: 212-869-2560 in New York State; 800-247-0909 elsewhere in the US).

Dialysis at Sea Cruises (611 Barry Pl., Indian Rocks Beach, FL 34635; phone: 800-775-1333 or 813-596-4614).

Evergreen Travel Service (4114 198th St. SW, Suite 13, Lynnwood, WA 98036-6742; phone: 800-435-2288 or 206-776-1184).

Flying Wheels Travel (143 W. Bridge St., PO Box 382, Owatonna, MN 55060; phone: 800-535-6790 or 507-451-5005).

Good Neighbor Travel Service (124 S. Main St., Viroqua, WI 54665; phone: 608-637-2128).

The Guided Tour (7900 Old York Rd., Suite 114B, Elkins Park, PA 19117-2339; phone: 800-783-5841 or 215-782-1370).

Hinsdale Travel (201 E. Ogden Ave., Hinsdale, IL 60521; phone: 708-325-1335 or 708-469-7349).

MedEscort International (ABE International Airport, PO Box 8766, Allentown, PA 18105; phone: 800-255-7182 or 215-791-3111).

Prestige World Travel (5710-X High Point Rd., Greensboro, NC 27407; phone: 800-476-7737 or 919-292-6690).

Sprout (893 Amsterdam Ave., New York, NY 10025; phone: 212-222-9575).

Weston Travel Agency (134 N. Cass Ave., PO Box 1050, Westmont, IL 60559; phone: 708-968-2513 in Illinois; 800-633-3725 elsewhere in the US).

Single Travelers

The travel industry is not very fair to people who vacation by themselves — they often end up paying more than those traveling in pairs.

Services catering to singles match travel companions, offer travel arrangements with shared accommodations, and provide useful information and discounts. Also consult publications such as *Going Solo* (Doerfer Communications, PO Box 123, Apalachicola, FL 32329; phone: 904-653-8848) and *Traveling on Your Own,* by Eleanor Berman (Random House, Order Dept., 400 Hahn Rd., Westminster, MD 21157; phone: 800-733-3000).

Organizations and Companies

Contiki Holidays (300 Plaza Alicante, Suite 900, Garden Grove, CA 92640; phone: 800-466-0610 or 714-740-0808).

Gallivanting (515 E. 79th St., Suite 20F, New York, NY 10021; phone: 800-933-9699 or 212-988-0617).

Globus and Cosmos (5301 S. Federal Circle, Littleton, CO 80123; phone: 800-221-0090 or 800-556-5454).

Jane's International and Sophisticated Women Travelers (2603 Bath Ave., Brooklyn, NY 11214; phone: 718-266-2045).

Marion Smith Singles (611 Prescott Pl., N. Woodmere, NY 11581; phone: 516-791-4852, 516-791-4865, or 212-944-2112).

Partners-in-Travel (11660 Chenault St., Suite 119, Los Angeles, CA 90049; phone: 310-476-4869).

Singles in Motion (545 W. 236th St., Riverdale, NY 10463; phone: 718-884-4464).

Singleworld (401 Theodore Fremd Ave., Rye, NY 10580; phone: 800-223-6490 or 914-967-3334).

Solo Flights (63 High Noon Rd., Weston, CT 06883; phone: 203-226-9993).

Suddenly Singles Tours (161 Dreiser Loop, Bronx, NY 10475; phone: 718-379-8800 in New York City; 800-859-8396 elsewhere in the US).

Travel Companion Exchange (PO Box 833, Amityville, NY 11701; phone: 516-454-0880).

Travel Companions (Atrium Financial Center, 1515 N. Federal Hwy., Suite 300, Boca Raton, FL 33432; phone: 800-383-7211 or 407-393-6448).

Travel in Two's (239 N. Broadway, Suite 3, N. Tarrytown, NY 10591; phone: 914-631-8301 in New York State; 800-692-5252 elsewhere in the US).

Older Travelers

Special discounts and more free time are just two factors that have given older travelers a chance to see the world at affordable prices. Many travel suppliers offer senior discounts — sometimes only to members of certain senior citizen organizations, which offer other benefits. Prepare your itinerary with one eye on your own physical condition and the other on a map, and remember that it's easy to overdo when traveling.

Publications

Going Abroad: 101 Tips for Mature Travelers (Grand Circle Travel, 347 Congress St., Boston, MA 02210; phone: 800-221-2610 or 617-350-7500).

The Mature Traveler (GEM Publishing Group, PO Box 50820, Reno, NV 89513-0820; phone: 702-786-7419).

Take a Camel to Lunch and Other Adventures for Mature Travelers, by Nancy O'Connell (Bristol Publishing Enterprises, PO Box 1737, San Leandro, CA 94577; phone: 510-895-4461 in California; 800-346-4889 elsewhere in the US).

Travel Tips for Older Americans (Publication #044-000-02270-2; Superintendent of Documents, US Government Printing Office, PO Box 371954, Pittsburgh, PA 15250-7954; phone: 202-783-3238).

Unbelievably Good Deals & Great Adventures That You Absolutely Can't Get Unless You're Over 50, by Joan Rattner Heilman (Contemporary Books, 180 N. Michigan Ave., Chicago, IL 60601; phone: 312-782-9181).

Organizations

American Association of Retired Persons (AARP; 601 E St. NW, Washington, DC 20049; phone: 202-434-2277).

Golden Companions (PO Box 754, Pullman, WA 99163-0754; phone: 208-858-2183).

Mature Outlook (Customer Service Center, 6001 N. Clark St., Chicago, IL 60660; phone: 800-336-6330).

National Council of Senior Citizens (1331 F St. NW, Washington, DC 20004; phone: 202-347-8800).

Package Tour Operators

Elderhostel (PO Box 1959, Wakefield, MA 01880-5959; phone: 617-426-7788).

Evergreen Travel Service (4114 198th St. SW, Suite 13, Lynnwood, WA 98036-6742; phone: 800-435-2288 or 206-776-1184).

Gadabout Tours (700 E. Tahquitz Canyon Way, Palm Springs, CA 92262; phone: 800-952-5068 or 619-325-5556).

Grand Circle Travel (347 Congress St., Boston, MA 02210; phone: 800-221-2610 or 617-350-7500).

Grandtravel (6900 Wisconsin Ave., Suite 706, Chevy Chase, MD 20815; phone: 800-247-7651 or 301-986-0790).

Interhostel (UNH Division of Continuing Education, 6 Garrison Ave., Durham, NH 03824; phone: 800-733-9753 or 603-862-1147).

OmniTours (104 Wilmont Rd., Deerfield, IL 60015; phone: 800-962-0060 or 708-374-0088).

Saga International Holidays (222 Berkeley St., Boston, MA 02116; phone: 800-343-0273 or 617-262-2262).

Money Matters

The basic unit of Mexican currency, the **peso,** is subdivided into 100 centavos. Paper bills *(billetes)* are issued in denominations of 1, 2, 5, 10, 20, 50, and 100 pesos, coins *(monedas)* in 5, 10, 20, and 50 centavos, and 1, 2, 5, and 10 pesos. These denominations apply to the new Mexican currency–called *nuevos pesos or N$* — issued on January 1, 1993 (pamphlets in English explaining this system are available at entry points). **WARNING: The new pesos (marked with "N$") are equal to 1,000 old pesos and should not be confused with old pesos (which may be in circulation at the time of your visit).**

Exchange rates are posted in international newspapers such as the *International Herald Tribune*. Foreign currency information and related services are provided by banks and companies such as *Thomas Cook Foreign Exchange* (for the nearest location, call 800-621-0666 or 312-236-0042), *Harold Reuter and Company* (200 Park Ave., Suite 332E, New York, NY 10166; phone: 212-661-0826), and *Ruesch International* (for the nearest location, call 800-424-2923 or 202-408-1200). In Mexico, you will find the official rate of exchange posted in banks, airports, money exchange houses, hotels, and some shops. Since you will get more pesos for your US dollar at banks and money exchanges, don't change more than $10 for foreign currency at other commercial establishments. Ask how much commission you're being charged and the exchange rate, and don't buy money on the black market (it may be counterfeit). Estimate your needs carefully; if you overbuy, you lose twice — buying and selling back.

TRAVELER'S CHECKS AND CREDIT CARDS

It's wise to carry traveler's checks while on the road, since they are replaceable if stolen or lost. You can buy traveler's checks at banks and some are available by mail or phone. Although most major credit cards enjoy wide domestic and international acceptance, not every hotel, restaurant, or shop in Cancún, Cozumel, or Isla Mujeres accepts all (or in some cases any) credit cards. When making purchases with a credit card, note that the rate of exchange depends on when the charge is processed; most credit card companies charge a 1% fee for converting foreign currency charges. Keep a separate list of all traveler's checks (noting those that you have cashed) and the names and numbers of your credit cards. Both traveler's check and credit card companies have international numbers to call for information or in the event of loss or theft.

CASH MACHINES

Automated teller machines (ATMs) are increasingly common worldwide. Most banks participate in one of the international ATM networks; cardholders can withdraw cash from any machine in the same network using either a "bank" card or, in some cases, a credit card. At the time of this writing, most ATMs belong to the *CIRRUS* or *PLUS* network. For further information, ask at your bank branch.

SENDING MONEY ABROAD

Should the need arise, it is possible to have money sent to you via the services provided by *American Express* (*MoneyGram;* phone: 800-926-9400 or 800-666-3997 for information; 800-866-8800 for money transfers) or *Western Union Financial Services* (phone: 800-325-4176).

If you are down to your last cent and have no other way to obtain cash, the nearest US Consulate will let you call home to set these matters in motion.

Accommodations

For specific information on hotels, resorts, and other selected accommodations, see THE ISLANDS and DIRECTIONS.

RENTAL OPTIONS

An attractive accommodations alternative for the visitor content to stay in one spot is to rent one of the numerous properties available throughout the Yucatán Peninsula. For a family or group, the per-person cost can be reasonable. To have your pick of the properties available, make inquiries at least 6 months in advance. The *Worldwide Home Rental Guide* (369 Montezuma, Suite 297, Santa Fe, NM 87501; phone: 505-984-7080) lists rental properties and managing agencies.

ACCOMMODATION DISCOUNTS

The following organizations offer discounts of up to 50% on accommodations throughout Mexico:

Entertainment Publishing (2125 Butterfield Rd., Troy, MI 48084; phone: 800-477-3234 or 313-637-8400).

International Travel Card (6001 N. Clark St., Chicago, IL 60660; phone: 800-342-0558 or 312-465-8891).

Privilege Card (5395 Roswell Rd., Suite 200, Atlanta, GA 30342; phone: 404-262-0222).

Quest International (402 E. Yakima Ave., Suite 1200, Yakima, WA 98901; phone: 800-325-2400 or 509-248-7512).

World Hotel Express (14900 Landmark Blvd., Suite 116, Dallas, TX

75240; phone: 800-866-2015 or 214-991-5482 for information; 800-580-2083 for reservations).

Time Zones

Cancún, Cozumel, and Isla Mujeres operate on central standard time and do not observe daylight saving time. Mexican timetables use a 24-hour clock to denote arrival and departure times, which means that hours are expressed sequentially from 1 AM.

Business Hours

Businesses often are open from 10 AM to 7 PM with a 2-hour break in the afternoon. Banks usually are open weekdays from 9 AM to 1:30 PM, and some also are open from 4 to 6 PM. Others may be open weekdays from 8:30 AM to 5 PM, and have weekend hours. Most money exchange houses *(cambios)* are open weekdays until 5 PM, and Saturdays until 2 PM; others stay open until 9 PM. Airport money exchanges are open on Sundays.

Holidays

Government offices, banks, and stores usually are closed on national holidays, as well as on the days just before and after. Many offices (but not banks) close between *Christmas* and *New Year's Day*. Following are the Mexican national holidays and the dates they will be observed this year:

January 1: *New Year's Day (Año Nuevo)*.
February 5: *Constitution Day*.
March 21: *Birthday of Benito Juárez*.
March 31: *Holy Thursday*.
April 1: *Good Friday*.
May 1: *Labor Day*.
May 5: Celebrates Mexico's victory over the French in 1862.
September 1: President's state of the union report *(Informe)* and the opening of Congress.
September 16: *Independence Day*.
October 11: *Columbus Day (Día de la Raza)*.
November 2: *All Souls' Day* (known in Mexico as the *Day of the Dead*).
November 20: Anniversary of the Mexican Revolution of 1910.
December 12: *Feast of Our Lady of Guadalupe*.
December 25: *Christmas*.
December 31: Banks closed for annual balance.

Mail

Always use airmail and allow at least 10 days for delivery between Cancún, Cozumel, and Isla Mujeres and the United States. Stamps are available at post offices, most hotel desks, and from public vending machines. Packages sent in Mexico should be registered. If your correspondence is especially important, you may want to send it via one of the international courier services, such as *Federal Express* or *DHL Worldwide Express*.

You can have mail sent to you care of your hotel (marked "Guest Mail, Hold for Arrival") or to a post office (the address should include "*a/c Lista de Correos*"). *American Express* offices also will hold mail for customers ("c/o Client Letter Service"); information is provided in their pamphlet *Travelers' Companion.* US Embassies and Consulates abroad will hold mail for US citizens *only* in emergency situations.

Telephone

Most Mexican cities and resort areas — including Cancún and Cozumel — have direct dialing to the US, although from some telephones you still may need the assistance of an international operator. Public telephones are widely available.

The procedure for calling Mexico from the US is to dial 011 (the international access code) + 52 (the country code) + the city code + the local number. (The city code for Cancún is 98; for Cozumel and Isla Mujeres it is 987.) To call the US from Mexico, dial 95 + the US area code + the local number. To make a call between Mexican cities, dial 91 + the city code + the local number. To call a number within the same city code coverage area, dial the local number.

You can use a telephone company credit card number on any phone, but pay phones that take special phone cards (called *Ladatel* phones) are increasingly common. Phone cards are sold at post offices, transportation and other commercial centers, and at some shops. Long-distance telephone services that help you avoid the surcharges that hotels routinely add to phone bills are provided by *American Telephone and Telegraph* (*AT&T Communications,* International Information Service, 635 Grant St., Pittsburgh, PA 15219; phone: 800-874-4000), *MCI* (323 3rd St. SE, Cedar Rapids, IA 52401; phone: 800-444-3333), *Metromedia Communications Corp.* (1 International Center, 100 NE Loop 410, San Antonio, TX 78216; phone: 800-275-0100), and *Sprint* (offices throughout the US; phone: 800-877-4000). Some hotels still may charge a fee for line usage.

AT&T's Language Line Service (phone: 800-752-6096) provides interpretive services for telephone communications in Spanish. Also useful are the *AT&T 800 Travel Directory* (available at *AT&T Phone Centers* or by calling 800-426-8686), the *Toll-Free Travel & Vacation Information Directory* (Pilot Books, 103 Cooper St., Babylon, NY 11702; phone: 516-422-

2225), and *The Phone Booklet* (*Scott American Corporation,* PO Box 88, W. Redding, CT 06896; phone: 203-938-2955).

Important Phone Numbers
Emergency assistance: 06
Long-distance operator: 02 (within Mexico)
International operator: 09 (English-speaking)
Local information: 04
Countrywide information: 01

Electricity

As in the US, Mexico uses 110-volt, 60-cycle, alternating current (AC). To be fully prepared, pack a wall socket adapter for any old outlets that have nonstandard plug configurations.

Staying Healthy

For information on current health conditions, call the Centers for Disease Control and Prevention's *International Health Requirements and Recommendations Information Hotline:* 404-332-4559. For travel to Mexico, the US Public Health Service advises diphtheria and tetanus shots; children also should be inoculated against measles, mumps, rubella, and polio.

To avoid intestinal upset (or infectious hepatitis), do not drink tap water in Mexico — do not even brush your teeth with it. Stick to bottled and canned drinks or use water purification tablets. Milk sold in stores is pasteurized and safe to drink, but beware of spoilage due to improper refrigeration. Avoid unpasteurized or uncooked dairy products, unpeeled fruit, or any uncooked vegetables. And do *not* buy food from street vendors.

When swimming, the undertow (a current running back down the beach after a wave has washed ashore) can knock you down, and riptides (currents running against the tide) can pull you out to sea. If you see a shark, swim away quietly and smoothly. Also beware of eels, Portuguese man-of-war (and other jellyfish), sea urchins, and razor-sharp coral reefs.

In well-developed resort areas such as Cancún and Cozumel, you will find thorough, well-trained specialists, and hospitals, clinics, and pharmacies with pretty much the same drugs as in the US (some available without a prescription). The quality of health care and the sophistication of medical facilities are less certain in rural and remote areas, and it often is best to arrange for transportation to the nearest metropolitan center. Ask at your hotel for the house physician or for help in reaching a doctor, or contact the US Consulate. Pharmacies may take turns staying open for 24 hours; contact a local hospital or medical clinic for information about on-call pharmacists.

Be extremely cautious about injections in Mexico because reusable syringes and needles are still common, and sterilization procedures may be inadequate. If you have a condition that requires occasional injections, bring a supply of syringes with you or buy disposable syringes.

In an emergency: Go to the emergency room of the nearest hospital, dial one of the emergency numbers given above, or call an operator for assistance.

Additional Resources

International Association of Medical Assistance to Travelers (IAMAT, 417 Center St., Lewiston, NY 14092; phone: 716-754-4883).

International Health Care Service (440 E. 69th St., New York, NY 10021; phone: 212-746-1601).

International SOS Assistance (PO Box 11568, Philadelphia, PA 19116; phone: 800-523-8930 or 215-244-1500).

Medic Alert Foundation (2323 Colorado Ave., Turlock, CA 95380; phone: 800-ID-ALERT or 209-668-3333).

TravMed (PO Box 10623, Baltimore, MD 21285-0623; phone: 800-732-5309 or 410-296-5225).

Consular Services

The American Services section of the US Consulate is a vital source of assistance and advice for US citizens abroad. If you are injured or become seriously ill, the Consulate can direct you to sources of medical attention and notify your relatives. If you become involved in a dispute that could lead to legal action, the Consulate is the place to turn. In cases of natural disasters or civil unrest, consulates handle the evacuation of US citizens if necessary.

The US Embassy is located in Mexico City (305 Paseo de la Reforma, Cuahtemoc, México, DF 06500; phone: 5-211-0042). There is a consular agent in Cancún (40 Av. Nader, #2A, Cancún, Quintana Roo; phone: 98-42411).

The US State Department operates a 24-hour *Citizens' Emergency Center* travel advisory hotline (phone: 202-647-5225). **In an emergency, call 202-647-4000 and ask for the duty officer.**

Entry Requirements and Customs Regulations

ENTERING MEXICO

A US citizen needs a tourist card and photo ID to travel to Cancún, Cozumel, and Isla Mujeres. To obtain a card, you must have proof of your

US citizenship: A passport alone will suffice; a birth certificate or voter's registration certificate must be accompanied by an official photo ID. A naturalized citizen needs either naturalization papers or an affidavit of citizenship (again with a photo ID). A minor under 18 traveling alone must have a passport and written permission from both parents or legal guardians or, if traveling with one guardian, a letter signed by the other (or proof of sole custody).

A tourist card can be obtained from Mexican Ministry of Tourism offices or Mexican Consulates in the US, Mexican government border offices, airline ticket offices, and some travel agencies. When you arrive in Mexico you must sign the card in the presence of the Mexican immigration official; proof of US citizenship may be required. The tourist card allows you to stay in Mexico for a specified period of time (the maximum is 6 months).

You are allowed to enter Mexico with the following duty-free: 2 liters of liquor, 1 carton of (200) cigarettes, a camera and a camcorder (plus film and/or video cartridges).

RETURNING TO THE US

You must declare to the US Customs official at the point of entry everything you have acquired in Mexico. The standard duty-free allowance for US citizens is $400; if your trip is shorter than 48 continuous hours, or you have been out of the US within 30 days, it is cut to $25. Families traveling together may make a joint declaration. The Generalized System of Preferences (which applies to Mexico) allows US citizens to bring certain goods into the US duty-free; antiques (at least 100 years old) and paintings or drawings done entirely by hand also are duty-free.

A flat 10% duty is assessed on the next $1,000 worth of merchandise; additional items are taxed at a variety of rates (see *Tariff Schedules of the United States* in a library or any US Customs Service office). With the exception of gifts valued at $50 or less sent directly to the recipient, items shipped home are dutiable. Some articles are duty-free only up to certain limits. The $400 allowance includes 1 carton of cigarettes, 100 cigars (not Cuban), and 1 liter of liquor or wine (for those over 21); the $25 allowance includes 10 cigars, 50 cigarettes, and 4 ounces of perfume. To avoid paying duty unnecessarily, before your trip, register the serial numbers of any expensive equipment you are bringing along with US Customs.

Forbidden imports include articles made of the furs or hides of animals on the endangered species list. In addition, you must obtain a permit from the *Instituto Nacional de Antropología e Historia* (45 Córdoba, Col. Roma, México, DF 06700; phone: 5-533-2263) to take original artifacts out of Mexico.

For further information, consult *Know Before You Go; International Mail Imports; Travelers' Tips on Bringing Food, Plant, and Animal Products into the United States; Importing a Car; GSP and the Traveler; Pocket*

Hints; Currency Reporting; and *Pets, Wildlife, US Customs,* all available from the US Customs Service (PO Box 7407, Washington, DC 20044). For tape-recorded information on travel-related topics, call 202-927-2095 from any touch-tone phone.

DUTY-FREE SHOPS Located in international airports, these provide bargains on purchases of foreign goods. But beware: Not all foreign goods are automatically less expensive. You *can* get a good deal on some items, but know what they cost elsewhere.

For Further Information

The Mexican government tourist offices in the US are the best sources of travel information. Offices generally are open on weekdays, during normal business hours; you also can call a 24-hour information hotline in Mexico City (phone: 915-250-0123, -0493, -0151, or -0589). Also consult the US Department of State's brochure *Tips for Travelers to Mexico* (Superintendent of Documents, US Government Printing Office, PO Box 371954, Pittsburgh, PA 15250-7954; phone: 202-783-3238).

Ministry of Tourism Offices
California: 10100 Santa Monica Blvd., Suite 224, Los Angeles, CA 90067 (phone: 310-203-8191).

Illinois: 70 E. Lake St., Suite 1413, Chicago, IL 60601 (phone: 312-565-2786).

New York: 405 Park Ave., Suite 1401, New York, NY 10022 (phone: 212-838-2949).

Texas: 2707 N. Loop W., Suite 450, Houston, TX 77008 (phone: 713-880-5153).

Washington, DC: 1911 Pennsylvania Ave. NW, Washington, DC 20006 (phone: 202-728-1750).

Useful Words and Phrases

Useful Words and Phrases

Unlike the French, who tend to be a bit brusque if you don't speak their language perfectly, the Mexicans do not expect you to speak Spanish, but appreciate your efforts when you try. In many circumstances, you won't have to, because the staffs at most hotels, museums, and tourist attractions, as well as at a fair number of restaurants, speak serviceable English, which they are eager to use. Off the beaten path, however, you will find at least a rudimentary knowledge of Spanish very helpful. Don't be afraid of misplaced accents or misconjugated verbs. Mexicans will do their best to understand you and will make every effort to be understood.

Mexican Spanish has a number of regional dialects, but the dialect of educated people in Mexico City is regarded as standard, is used on national television, and is understood by almost everybody. The spelling of standard Mexican Spanish is a very reliable guide to pronunciation.

The list below of commonly used words and phrases can help you get started.

Greetings and Everyday Expressions

Good morning (also, Good day).	*Buenos días*
Good afternoon/evening	*Buenas tardes*
Good night	*Buenas noches*
Hello	*Hola!*
How are you?	*Cómo está usted?*
Pleased to meet you	*Mucho gusto en conocerle*
Good-bye!	*Adiós!*
So long!	*Hasta luego!*
Yes	*Sí*
No	*No*
Please	*Por favor*
Thank you	*Gracias*
You're welcome	*De nada*
I beg your pardon (Excuse me).	*Perdón*
I'm sorry	*Lo siento*
It doesn't matter	*No importa*
I don't speak Spanish.	*No hablo Español.*
Do you speak English?	*Habla usted inglés?*
I don't understand.	*No comprendo.*
Do you understand?	*Comprende?/Entiende?*

My name is . . .	*Me llamo . . .*
What is your name?	*Cómo se llama?*
miss	*señorita*
madame	*señora* (married).
	doña (unmarried).
mister	*señor*
open	*abierto/a*
closed	*cerrado/a*
entrance	*entrada*
exit	*salida*
push	*empujar*
pull	*jalar*
today	*hoy*
tomorrow	*mañana*
yesterday	*ayer*

Checking In

I have a reservation.	*Tengo una reservación.*
I would like . . .	*Quisiera . . .*
a single room	*una habitación sencilla*
a double room	*una habitación doble*
a quiet room	*una habitación tranquila*
with bath	*con baño*
with shower	*con ducha*
with a sea view	*con vista al mar*
with air conditioning	*con aire acondicionado*
with balcony	*con balcón*
overnight only	*sólo una noche*
a few days	*unos cuantos días*
a week (at least)	*una semana (por lo menos)*
with full board	*con pensión completa*
with half board	*con media pensión*
Does that price include	*Está incluído en el precio*
breakfast?	*el desayuno?*
taxes?	*los impuestos?*
Do you accept traveler's checks?	*Acepta usted cheques de viajero?*
Do you accept credit cards?	*Acepta tarjetas de crédito?*
It doesn't work.	*No funciona.*

Eating Out

ashtray	*un cenicero*
(extra) chair	*una silla (adicional)*
table	*una mesa*
bottle	*una botella*

cup	*una taza*
plate	*un plato*
fork	*un tenedor*
knife	*un cuchillo*
spoon	*una cuchara*
napkin	*una servilleta*
hot chocolate (cocoa)	*un chocolate caliente*
black coffee	*un café negro*
coffee with milk	*café con leche*
cream	*crema*
milk	*leche*
tea	*un té*
fruit juice	*un jugo de fruta*
lemonade	*una limonada*
water	*agua*
mineral water	*agua mineral*
carbonated	* con gas*
noncarbonated	* sin gas*
orangeade	*una naranjada*
beer	*una cerveza*
port	*oporto*
sherry	*jerez*
red wine	*vino tinto*
white wine	*vino blanco*
cold	*frío/a*
hot	*caliente*
sweet	*dulce*
(very) dry	*(muy) seco/a*
bread	*pan*
butter	*mantequilla*
bacon	*tocino*
eggs	*huevos*
hard-boiled	* un huevo cocido*
fried	* huevos fritos*
omelette	* un omelette*
soft-boiled	* un huevo pasado por agua*
scrambled	* huevos revueltos*
honey	*miel*
jam, marmalade	*mermelada*
orange juice	*jugo de naranja*
pepper	*pimienta*

salt	*sal*
sugar	*azúcar*
Waiter!	*Camarero!/Mesero!*
I would like	*Quisiera*
a glass of	*un vaso de*
a bottle of	*una botella de*
a half bottle of	*una media botella de*
a carafe of	*una jarra de*
a liter of	*un litro de*
The check, please.	*La cuenta, por favor.*
Is a service charge included?	*Está el servicio incluido?*
I think there is a mistake in the bill.	*Creo que hay un error en la cuenta.*

Shopping

bakery	*la panadería*
bookstore	*la librería*
butcher shop	*la carnicería*
camera shop	*la tienda de fotografía*
department store	*el almacén*
grocery	*la tienda de comestibles*
jewelry store	*la joyería*
newsstand	*el puesto de periódicos*
pastry shop	*la pastelería*
perfume (and cosmetics) store	*perfumería*
pharmacy/drugstore	*la farmacia*
shoestore	*la zapatería*
supermarket	*el supermercado*
tobacconist	*la tabaquería*
inexpensive	*barato/a*
expensive	*caro/a*
large	*grande*
larger	*más grande*
too large	*demasiado grande*
small	*pequeño/a*
smaller	*más pequeño/a*
too small	*demasiado pequeño/a*
long	*largo/a*
short	*corto/a*
old	*viejo/a*
new	*nuevo/a*
used	*usado/a*
handmade	*hecho/a a mano*

Is it machine washable?	*Es lavable en lavadora?*
How much does it cost?	*Cuánto cuesta esto?*
What is it made of?	*De qué está hecho?*
camel's hair	*pelo de camello*
cotton	*algodón*
corduroy	*pana*
filigree	*filigrana*
lace	*encaje*
leather	*cuero*
linen	*lino*
suede	*ante*
synthetic	*sintético/a*
tile	*baldosa*
wood	*madera*
wool	*lana*
brass	*latón*
copper	*cobre*
gold	*oro*
gold plated	*dorado*
silver	*plata*
silver plated	*plateado*
stainless steel	*acero inoxidable*

Colors

beige	*beige*
black	*negro/a*
blue	*azul*
brown	*café*
green	*verde*
gray	*gris*
orange	*anaranjado/a*
pink	*rosa*
purple	*morado/a*
red	*rojo/a*
white	*blanco/a*
yellow	*amarillo/a*
dark	*obscuro/a*
light	*claro/a*

Getting Around

north	*norte*
south	*sur*
east	*este*
west	*oeste*

right	derecho/a
left	izquierdo/a
Go straight ahead.	Siga todo derecho.
far	lejos
near	cerca
gas station	la gasolinería
train station	la estación de ferrocarril
bus stop	la parada de autobuses
subway station	estación de metro
airport	el aeropuerto
tourist information	información turística
map	el mapa
one-way ticket	un boleto de ida
round-trip ticket	un boleto de ida y vuelta
track	el andén
first class	primera clase
second class	segunda clase
smoking	fumar
no smoking	no fumar
gasoline	gasolina
regular	nova
premium	extra
leaded	con plomo
unleaded	magna sin or sin plomo
diesel	diesel
Fill it up, please.	Llénelo, por favor.
oil	el aceite
tires	las llantas
Where is . . . ?	Dónde está . . . ?
Where are . . . ?	Dónde están . . . ?
How far is it from here to . . . ?	Qué distancia hay desde aquí hasta . . . ?
Does this train go to . . . ?	Va este tren a . . . ?
Does this bus go to . . . ?	Va este autobús a . . . ?
What time does it leave?	A qué hora sale?
Danger	Peligro
Caution	Precaución
Detour	Desviación
Do Not Enter	Paso Prohibido
No Parking	Estacionamiento Prohibido
No Passing	Prohibido Pasar
One Way	Dirección Unica

Pay Toll	Peaje
Pedestrian Zone	Zona Peatonal
Reduce Speed	Despacio
Steep Incline	Fuerte Declive
Stop	Alto
Use Headlights	Encender los faros
Yield	Ceda el Paso

Personal Items and Services

aspirin	aspirina
Band-Aids	curitas
barbershop	la peluquería
beauty shop	el salón de belleza
condom	condón
dry cleaner	la tintorería
hairdresser's	la peluquería
laundromat	la lavandería
laundry	la lavandería
post office	el correo
postage stamps	timbres
sanitary napkins	toallas femininas
shampoo	un champú
shaving cream	espuma de afeitar
soap	el jabón
tampons	unos tampones
tissues	Kleenex
toilet paper	papel higiénico
toothpaste	pasta de dientes
Where is the bathroom?	Dónde está el baño?
toilet?	tocador?
MEN	Caballeros
WOMEN	Señoras

Days of the Week

Monday	Lunes
Tuesday	Martes
Wednesday	Miércoles
Thursday	Jueves
Friday	Viernes
Saturday	Sábado
Sunday	Domingo

Months

January	Enero
February	Febrero
March	Marzo

April	*Abril*
May	*Mayo*
June	*Junio*
July	*Julio*
August	*Agosto*
September	*Septiembre*
October	*Octubre*
November	*Noviembre*
December	*Diciembre*

Numbers

zero	*cero*
one	*uno*
two	*dos*
three	*tres*
four	*cuatro*
five	*cinco*
six	*seis*
seven	*siete*
eight	*ocho*
nine	*nueve*
ten	*diez*
eleven	*once*
twelve	*doce*
thirteen	*trece*
fourteen	*catorce*
fifteen	*quince*
sixteen	*dieciséis*
seventeen	*diecisiete*
eighteen	*dieciocho*
nineteen	*diecinueve*
twenty	*veinte*
thirty	*treinta*
forty	*cuarenta*
fifty	*cincuenta*
sixty	*sesenta*
seventy	*setenta*
eighty	*ochenta*
ninety	*noventa*
one hundred	*cien*
one thousand	*mil*

The Islands

Cancún
(pronounced Cahn-*koon*)

For many years, small groups of divers and determined sun worshipers had the lagoons, beaches, and islands of Mexico's Caribbean Coast along the Yucatán Peninsula almost to themselves. People planning a trip to the Yucatán had to choose among the Maya ruins at Chichén Itzá, Uxmal, and Tulum, sun and sea sports along the coast of Quintana Roo, including Xel-Ha (pronounced Shell-*ha*) and Akumal; or the islands of Isla Mujeres, Cancún, or Cozumel. Transportation was too difficult to make all sides of the vacation coin easily accessible. About the only visitors who had enough time to do it all were the wealthy divers who belonged to private clubs tucked away in silent lagoons along the coast and who flew private planes into the Yucatán.

In those days, Mexico's largest island, Cozumel, was the preferred Caribbean destination of less well heeled travelers. They flew into Mérida, grabbed a plane to Cozumel, and flopped there on the sand for several days of swimming, diving, fishing, and lots and lots of lazing. Cancún was an undeveloped spit of land off the coast to the north.

No more. All that changed when FONATUR, the government agency charged with improving Mexico's tourist facilities, chose Cancún as its first multimillion-dollar experiment in resort development. It was discovered that Cancún had all the natural attributes of a resort area — beautiful sea and some of the best diving in the world, adequate space and facilities, proximity to the ruins — and FONATUR proceeded without hesitation. So new it wasn't even marked on road maps in 1970, Cancún has blossomed into one of the world's most bustling — and some feel over-developed — young resorts. By next year, the city expects to welcome 2.8 million visitors.

In reality Cancún is a Caribbean island — more a sandbar shaped like an emaciated sea horse — 14 miles long and a quarter mile wide, connected by a causeway at its nosepoint to Cancún City, the support city on the mainland where over 300,000 people now live. For most of the island's length, island and peninsula are separated by unruffled Nichupté Lagoon. Most of the island's resort hotels are scattered along the skinny east–west sand spit that forms the sea horse's head. Along its back, the Caribbean surf rolls in along a 12-mile length of shore with intermittent stretches of powdery white beach. There are a couple of commercial hotels in Cancún City, catering mostly to business travelers, but good for budget travelers as well, and there are some pleasant hotels with pools that offer free transportation to and from the beach. And it looks even more prosperous for Cancún City. Slated for development is the $600-million Malecón Cancún, a 330-acre project that will include homes, shops, restaurants, offices, and a park overlooking the lagoon and Cancún's Hotel Zone.

One of the major dividends of the development at Cancún is that travelers no longer have to choose between culture and carousal. Part of the Cancún master plan — a 15-year program of development — is a system of roads, transportation, and communications that connects the resort area to the major ruins and Mérida. Both Cancún and Cozumel benefit from a beeline road from the sea to Chichén Itzá, along which tour buses roll daily. And both are helped by the improvement of the shoreline road to Xel-Ha and the small but interesting ruins at Tulum and Cobá.

But the sea is still the major attraction. The crystalline Caribbean offers visibility to 100 feet, and the stretch of sea along the peninsula is world-famous as an area rich in fish, wrecks, and coral. Nichupté Lagoon is protected from the open sea. But the government poured some $100 million into the area to assure a complete resort infrastructure: recreational facilities like the 18-hole Robert Trent Jones, Jr. golf course, ships for touring, boats for sailing, and a panoply of hotels. Paseo Kukulcán, the boulevard running from one end of Cancún to the other, has been expanded from two lanes to four. Currently there are over 80 hotels in operation in both Cancún and Cancún City, plus condominiums, shopping centers, restaurants and marinas scattered along Kukulcán. In addition, the recently renovated, 12,000-seat convention center includes facilities for musical and theatrical performances. Cancún's weather and facilities are an authentic lure, but this is not the place for those who prize peace and privacy.

Cozumel
(pronounced Co-zoo-*mehl*)

Although it was the first island to be developed in the area, Cozumel has grown at a much slower pace than Cancún, and tends to attract visitors who are more interested in skin diving and fishing than in the glamour and nightlife of its glitzier neighbor. Plans for several new hotels were dropped because of potential threats to the island's ecological system — not to mention its tranquillity.

Everything moves at a slower pace in Cozumel. Whether strolling, cycling, or touring the island in a rented jeep, you can relax and take in the scenery without the distractions of Cancún's big-city milieu.

Eleven miles off the mainland coast, Cozumel is Mexico's largest island. A favorite haunt of undersea explorer Jacques Cousteau, the island's guest registry also boasts the names of Queen Elizabeth II of England and King Gustav of Sweden. According to local accounts, Charles A. Lindbergh flew Anne Morrow to the island during their courtship in the late 1920s.

The name Cozumel comes from the Maya phrase *cuzam huzil,* which means "land of the swallows." For over 12 centuries, Cozumel was the exclusive domain of the Maya. As early as AD 300, this 33-mile-long island was the site of a shrine to the lunar and fertility goddess Ix-chel, who benevolently watched over weavers and pregnant women but, when angered, released her wrath through violent hurricanes and torrential rains.

Spanish sea captain Gonzalo Guerrero is credited with having been the first European to set foot on Cozumel, when he drifted ashore after being shipwrecked in 1511. Legend has it that Guerrero married the daughter of a local chieftain and introduced the Maya to Western culture. Seven years later, Hernán Cortés and Juan de Grijalva claimed Cozumel for the Spanish crown, bringing with them the plague of smallpox, which essentially eradicated the island's population.

For the next 300 years, Cozumel remained almost uninhabited, except for the occasional pirate ship or adventure seeker who stumbled ashore in hopes of finding lost treasures. It was not until the mid-1800s that Cozumel was finally repopulated by Maya refugees fleeing persecution during the brutal Castes War.

During World War II, the US government used Cozumel as a military airfield and supply base. GIs stationed on the island during that time were, perhaps, the first Americans to discover its underwater attractions.

Today, Cozumel is a scuba diver's paradise, with underwater visibility commonly reaching 250 feet and subaquatic scenery that includes black coral and hundreds of species of tropical fish. Palancar, its main coral reef, is the second-largest natural coral formation in the world. To preserve their beauty, all the reefs surrounding the island have been declared national parks by the Mexican government.

Fishermen are also drawn to Cozumel, where the channel between the mainland and the island — populated with marlin, sailfish, grouper, mackerel, and other species — runs as deep as 600 feet. With catches of up to 120 pounds, several world sailfish records have been set on Cozumel.

With a total population of just over 60,000, the island has only one town, San Miguel, which serves simultaneously as the main seaport, commercial center, and restaurant zone. Most of Cozumel's hotels are spread to the left and right of town along the main road, which loops around the southern coastline.

Isla Mujeres
(pronounced *Ees*-lah Moo-*hair*-ehs)

Words like "quaint," "casual," and "easygoing" may never be applied to a super-resort like Cancún, but just across the bay from this island is Isla Mujeres, just 5 miles long and a half-mile wide, and situated 6 miles off Puerto Juárez on the Yucatán Peninsula. Unlike Cancún, Isla Mujeres — with its few charming, but fairly simple, hotels and wide expanses of beach — is an unpretentious little fishing village where things move at a turtle's pace and informality is the order of the day. Most places have phones and there are a few paved roads, but its tiny town, lagoons, reefs, and transparent waters make it a pleasant retreat for snorkelers, skin divers, and loafers.

The name Isla Mujeres (Isle of Women) was coined by the first Spaniards who set foot on this easternmost corner of Mexico. It seems that the ancient Maya had used the island for ceremonial purposes and had left life-size statues of their goddesses to ward off hurricanes from the sea. While the deities may have been successful in protecting the island from inclement weather, their powers did not save Isla Mujeres from falling into European hands. By 1520, the island was owned and controlled by the conquistadores.

Isla Mujeres, then known as "Dolores," was a vital lookout point for the Spanish, but offered little economically. It did, however, become a favorite haunt for pirates and criminals alike. One of the island's most notorious pirates was Fermín Mundaca, a slave trader, who fell in love with a native girl; in an effort to win her favor the buccaneer presented her with a magnificent mansion on beautifully landscaped grounds. The girl rejected him, fleeing instead with a younger man, and the old pirate mourned his unrequited love to his death. Today, the crumbling ruins of Mundaca's mansion have been reclaimed by the Mexican government, which plans to convert the grounds into an ecological reserve.

Isla Mujeres is a long strip of rocky beach that was once connected to the country's mainland but broke away millions of years ago. Mujeres Bay, a pale green gauntlet that runs between Puerto Juárez and Isla Mujeres, is actually a large sea canal. Once scarcely populated, the island today has 14,000 inhabitants, who live in the tiny village of Isla at the northern tip. This growth has been a direct result of the rise in tourism during the past 10 years. The rest of Isla Mujeres is nothing more than open spaces with an occasional fishing hut or a resort restaurant operated by one of the many cruisers that carry visitors from Cancún each day.

The island's most famous attraction is El Garrafón, an underwater national park located at the southern end and renowned for its coral reef and tropical fish. It's a great place to snorkel or dive, but it can't compete with Palancar Reef.

Cancún, Cozumel, and Isla Mujeres At-a-Glance

SEEING THE ISLANDS

The best way to get a bird's-eye view of all three islands is from *Pelican Pier Avioturismo*'s ultra-light seaplane that takes off from Cancún's lagoon for a 15-minute flight over the Hotel Zone (phone: 830315 or 831935). Kukulcán Boulevard is the only street on Cancún Island. In mainland Cancún City, Avenida Tulum is the main drag, but Avenida Yaxchilan is shaping up as the address of the more fashionable shops and restaurants. The village of San Miguel on Cozumel is about 10 blocks long and a few blocks wide; with many shops, restaurants, and boutiques, it offers much to see and savor. Isla Mujeres has plenty of choice seafood restaurants, and some of the finest handicrafts for sale, along the streets near the main plaza.

SPECIAL PLACES

Cancún is spread out, but there are lots of ways to get around. Taxis are plentiful, city bus service is good, and cars, motor scooters, and bicycles are available for rent. Also, open-air wooden buses now run from the Hotel Zone to downtown. There are regular bus and boat tours to several areas along with scheduled air service to more distant points and charters from *Pelican Pier Avioturismo* (phone: 830315 or 831935). You can easily tour the little village of San Miguel on foot or drive around the rest of Cozumel. The best way to get around Isla Mujeres is simply to walk. If you prefer, rent a bike or moped to whisk you to the nearest secluded beach or the beautiful national park, El Garrafón.

CANCÚN

BEACHES Many of the hotels on the island are on the beach; the beaches themselves, however, are federal property, so anyone can use them. The most popular public beach on the island is called Chac-Mool, and it is lovely. The "back side" of the island faces out on calm, lovely lagoons, favorite spots for divers and novice swimmers (see also *Swimming and Sunning* in this chapter).

CRUISES Any number of voyages may be made from Cancún or nearby points. If getting there is half the fun, you might prefer a leisurely crossing to Isla Mujeres on the *Tropical Cruiser,* which includes a full-day tour replete with a buffet lunch, soft drinks, musical show, and a snorkeling trip to El Garrafón for about $30. It sails Mondays through Saturdays at 10 AM from Playa Langosta dock (phone: 831488). Other cruises to Isla Mujeres include the *Tropical Cruiser Morning Express,* with a price of $15 for snorkeling and a hearty buffet meal (phone: 831488); the *Aqua Quin* trimaran (phone: 831883), which offers daily sails with a no-frills package of snacks and snorkeling priced at $35; and the *Nautibus Yellow Submarine* (phone: 832119 or 833602), where for $25 you can explore the local underwater flora and fauna while comfortably seated inside its windowed keel. But without a doubt, the classiest act on the Mexican Caribbean waters is the *Corsario* (phone: 830200), a motorized 50-foot replica of an 18th-century pirate ship that sets sail daily for Isla Mujeres from Playa Linda pier. Cost, including a seafood lunch, is $40.

The *México,* billed as the world's largest water jet, makes the round trip ten times daily to Cozumel; cost is about $10 one-way. Water jets leave from Playa del Carmen (phone: in Cozumel, 21508 or 21588). *Aviomar* (phone: 848831 or 848841; fax: 845385) offers the Escape to Cozumel tour, which leaves Playa Linda pier daily at 9 AM via bus and water jet to Cozumel; the day includes sightseeing, swimming, refreshments, and lunch on the beach for about $75.

There are also many private boats, ranging in size from tiny fishing launches to seagoing 40-footers, which can be chartered for a fee. Check with your hotel travel desk for details (see also *Boating* in this chapter).

EL REY These modest Maya ruins on the lagoon at the southern end of the island are hardly impressive compared with those at Tulum or Cobá, let alone Chichén Itzá, but they are worth a visit. When they were first excavated in the 1950s, the skeleton of a relatively large human male was discovered on top of the site's box-like central temple. There were also scattered remains of other bodies which apparently were sacrificed at the same time. Some anthropologists suggest that the main skeleton was that of a chieftain (hence the name "rey," king in Spanish). Unfortunately, because the site had been sacked by looters before its discovery, there are too few surviving vestiges to determine with certainty just what purpose this temple served in ancient Maya times.

YAMIL LU'UM It's easy to miss these two squat temples next to the *Camino Real* hotel. Dating from about AD 1300, they seem to have been watchtowers for the maritime Maya. Although archaeologically they are of little importance by themselves, their presence here indicates the breadth of the ancient Maya empire.

EL CASTILLO A small replica of El Castillo Pyramid (the original is in Chichén Itzá) sits at the head of *Plaza Caracol*. Every night, except Tuesdays, the phenomenon of the spring and fall equinoxes is re-created with a spectacular light show. The lights actually produce illusionary shadows of a serpent's body leading from the temple on top to the carved head on the bottom. The show in Spanish begins at 7 PM; in English, at 8 and 9 PM. Admission charge.

COZUMEL

COZUMEL MUSEUM The museum features impressive 3-D models of tropical fish, man-eating sharks, and underwater caves in the offshore reefs; as well as historical and ethnographical exhibits. There's also a library, temporary exhibits, a restaurant, and crafts shop. Open from 10 AM to 6 PM; closed Saturdays. Admission charge. On Rafael Melgar between Calles 4 and 6. (phone: 21545).

PLAZA The heart of Cozumel is a wide plaza near where the ferry docks, a spot everyone manages to find. Most of the shops and restaurants are here. Motor scooter renters must be careful not to park on the plaza; parking is forbidden and "motos" may be hauled off to scooter prison — and you'll be inconvenienced by having to pay the fine and arrange for their release.

CHANKANAB LAGOON AND BOTANICAL GARDENS About 5 miles (8 km) south of town, it's something of a natural aquarium filled with multicolored tropical fish. However, since suntan lotion collects in the water and harms the fish, swimming and snorkeling are not permitted in the lagoon (but are allowed at the nearby beach). The gardens boast over 400 species of tropical plants. Open daily from 7 AM to 5 PM. Admissions is $3.

SAN FRANCISCO BEACH On the southern tip of Cozumel, the island's best beach now can be reached by paved road, but it's also fun getting there aboard one of the vessels making the *El Zorro* cruise (phone: 20831). If you're not on a cruise that provides lunch, either of the two seafood restaurants here is a good choice.

PUNTA MORENA At this beach on the open Caribbean side of the island, the surf is rougher and swimming can be dangerous. There's a thatch-hut restaurant out this way, a good place to try grilled fish and a beer.

CELARAIN LIGHTHOUSE On the southeast tip of Cozumel, this lighthouse offers a spectacular view of the entire island.

ISLA MUJERES

EL GARRAFÓN Located at the island's southern end, this underwater national park is the island's most famous attraction. Renowned for its coral reef and tropical fish, it's a great place to snorkel or dive, but it can't compete with Palancar Reef. There's also a sea museum with an aquarium and pieces of wrecked historic galleons.

CAVES OF THE SLEEPING SHARKS Those with a thirst for danger will be drawn here: It's about the only place on earth where these man-eating beasts will sit still for human caresses. See also *Quintessential Cancún, Cozumel, and the Yucatán* in DIVERSIONS.

EXCURSIONS

CONTOY ISLAND Declared a National Wildlife Reserve in 1961, Contoy is a tiny, completely undeveloped coral island 25 miles (40 km) north of Cancún. A favorite destination for bird watchers, it is home to gulls, pelicans, petrels, cormorants, herons, frigates, and spoonbills. And although there are well over 100 species, their numbers are dwindling every day. It's also an important migratory point for other birds, and an egg-laying spot for sea turtles. Warning: If you should happen upon a sea turtle, look but don't touch! Disturbing these creatures is considered a very serious crime in Mexico, punishable by a long jail sentence.

The only structures on the island are a small visitor's center (with primitive restrooms) with an open-air exhibit on the island's flora and fauna, and an observation tower that offers fabulous views of the lush mangroves and lagoons. An afternoon on Contoy can be pleasantly spent simply lying on the narrow and nearly deserted beach on the island's leeward shore; swimming and snorkeling (although the visibility can be less than crystal clear at times) in the warm water; taking a boat ride (for an additional fee) into the island's interior lagoons, where bird nesting areas are quite visible; or simply exploring on your own. The interior parts of this island are lush, and although there are some paths, most beach-combers follow the shore past the main beach to discover tiny coves studded with conch shells. Hardly the place for thrill seekers, Contoy Island offers pristine beaches and an untouched landscape.

Cruises leave from Isla Mujeres and Cancún for the approximately 2-hour journey to Contoy (check with your hotel desk or local tourist board for departure times); cost is about $60 per person, which includes a tasty lunch of freshly caught and grilled fish, and chicken and rice with ceviche. Be sure to ask for the tequila "slammers" on the way home. During the excursion, you'll have the opportunity to snorkel in the calm waters, or perhaps try your hand at fishing (equipment can be rented for about $5). *Cooperativa Transporte Turística* (phone: 20274 on Isla Mujeres) offers prearranged package tours leaving from Isla Mujeres for about $40; the cost includes a light breakfast, lunch, and snorkeling equipment.

The *Contoy II* also offers all-day trips to the island from the Playa Linda Dock in Cancún. Cruises, which cost about $50 per person with lunch and drinks, depart at 9 AM Mondays through Saturdays (phone: 871909 or 871862).

AKUMAL One of the best snorkeling and scuba diving spots along Mexico's Caribbean Coast, Akumal is 59 miles (94 km) south of Cancún — and 18 miles (29 km) south of Playa del Carmen, the port closest to Cozumel — on Route 307. Once headquarters of a private club run by undersea explorers in search of treasure from the Spanish Main, Akumal now has an underwater museum where anchors and guns encrusted in coral lie among the rocks, much the way they originally were discovered.

Stops along Route 307 on the way to Akumal include Crococún, Mexico's only crocodile farm, and a biological research center, 20 miles (32 km) south of Cancún; the charming beach of Punta Beté (12 miles/19 km south of Crococún), where thousands of sea turtles lay their eggs every spring — as they do in Paamul, about 19 miles (30 km) farther south; and the sun-kissed beach, cenote (sinkhole), and ruins of Xcaret (13 miles/21 km south of Punta Beté, between Playa del Carmen and Paamul). Also along the route is the rapidly growing high-priced resort of Puerto Aventuras (just 3 miles/5 km south of Paamul and 5 miles/8 km north of Akumal), which already features the largest marina in Mexico, an 18-hole golf course, tennis courts, and a marine archaeology center whose collection includes relics salvaged from a Spanish ship that sank off the coast in 1741. There is also a luxury complex with villa-like suites, a pool, and a restaurant. Playacar, a recently built mega-resort adjacent to Playa del Carmen, boasts two luxury hotels, and an 18-hole golf course.

If you continue 6 miles (10 km) south of Akumal, a sign welcomes you to Chemuyil, "the most beautiful beach in the world." Also nearby is Xel-Ha, a lagoon that is a natural aquarium.

XEL-HA Although not nearly as crystal clear as it once was, this natural aquarium is a good place to test your snorkeling mask and fins before heading into the deeper waters at Palancar.

Xel-Ha is just north of Tulum on Route 307 to Chetumal.

EXTRA SPECIAL Tulum, a once thriving Maya center — built on a cliff above the sea and thought to be a major port and religious center — remains a place of mystery. Apparently inhabited at the time of the Spanish conquest, when other ceremonial cities had been abandoned, it was fortified and surrounded by a great wall. Tulum reached its apogee between AD 1000 and 1600, during the decline of the Maya civilization, and lacks the magnitude of such earlier cities as Chichén Itzá and Uxmal. The buildings found at Tulum are comparatively small in scale. However, the setting of Tulum — overlooking the fine white beaches and crystalline blue waters of the Caribbean — is magnificent and the trip should not be missed. The ruins are about 81 miles (129 km) from Cancún, with which it is connected by daily bus service. Admission charge.

Discovered in 1897, with excavations begun in 1973, Cobá was one of the largest cities in the Yucatán, covering about 40 square miles. It is thought to have been a trade center and, like Tulum, a religious center with a population of 50,000 and was connected by a network of highways with other major Maya cities such as Chichén Itzá and Uxmal. About a half-mile (1 km) south of Tulum is a road that heads 26 miles (42 km) inland to this fascinating jungle-bound site on the banks of an island lagoon.

Extending south of Tulum to Punta Allen is Sian Ka'an, a 1.3-million-acre biosphere reserve, containing tropical forests, mangrove swamps, salt marshes, palm-rimmed beaches, archaeological ruins, and coral reefs, which combines the protection of wildlife with the balanced use of its resources. It's a paradise for bird watchers and crocodile and butterfly lovers. If you venture far enough into the jungle (not recommended as a solo journey), you're likely to come across a jaguar or some other member of the large cat species. There are two fine hotels on the reserve, where you also are likely to run into some millionaire yachtsmen cruising the Caribbean: the pricey *Club de Pesca Boca Paila* (represented by *Carltony Tours,* A.P. 59, Cozumel, Q.R.; phone: 987-20053; 800-245-1950 in the US) and the *Pez Maya* (fax: 987-20072 on Cozumel; 800-327-2880 in the US). Considerably more rustic accommodations are available at *El Retiro* at Punta Xamach (clean cabins, but no private baths), or at the *Cuzan* guesthouse at Punta Allen (thatch palm tepees). In Punta Allen, Sonia Lopez will provide a good meal, but only if you ask nicely, and arrangements can be made with one of the fishermen to visit *los cayos* (the keys). For guided visits, contact the *Association of Friends of Sian Ka'an* (Plaza Américas, Suite 50, Cancún, Q.R. 77500; phone: 849583; fax: 873080). For further information on Cobá and Sian Ka'an, see *The Yucatán Peninsula: Cancún to Chetumal,* DIRECTIONS.

Sources and Resources

TOURIST INFORMATION

The best sources of information on Cancún are a pocket-size, biannual magazine, *Cancún Tips,* and the quarterly *Cancún Tips* magazine, both available in many hotel rooms or on sale around town. *Cozumel in One Day* and the *Blue Guide to Cozumel* also provide up-to-date information about that island. On Isla Mujeres, the *Islander* tells you what's going on. Hotel travel desks are other good sources. The Quintana Roo Tourist Office is in the FONATUR Building at Cobá and Nader (phone: 843238; fax: 843438), and there's an information booth on Avenida Tulum and Tulipanes, near the *Ki-Huic Market* (phone: 848073). Hotel personnel are also very helpful. On Cozumel, the tourist office (phone: 20972) is in the Plaza del Sol Building, and there is an information booth on the main square and at the tourist dock. The Isla Mujeres Tourist Office is at 6 Hidalgo (phone: 70188).

LOCAL COVERAGE The *News,* an English-language daily, is flown in from Mexico City; its Sunday travel supplement, *Vistas,* often carries reports on Cancún and Cozumel.

TELEPHONE

The city code for Cancún is 98; Cozumel and Isla Mujeres is 987. When calling from a phone on Cancún, Cozumel, or Isla Mujeres, use only the local number unless otherwise indicated.

GETTING AROUND

BUS Cancún probably has the best municipal bus service in Mexico. Routes follow a straight line, and the vehicles are seldom crowded. Transfers between the airport and hotels are handled by a fleet of minibuses that depart promptly, handle all luggage, and charge about $5 per person.

From 6 AM until midnight, another bus flock covers the distance between Cancún City and the Tourist Zone's hotels and shopping area; fare is about 75¢. There are also FONATUR buses — with reclining seats and air conditioning — which cost about $1. Buses run along the island, passing all the hotels, and go on into the city. Buses also go out to Puerto Juárez, where the ferries leave for Isla Mujeres. Intercity buses, *Autotransportes del Caribe* (*ADC;* phone: 841378), and *Autotransportes del Oriente* (*ADO;* phone: 843301) offer four departures daily for Akumal, Tulum, and Chetumal. There are ten departures each day for Chichén Itzá and Mérida.

CAR RENTAL In Cancún City, several agencies offer rental cars and jeeps for about $35 up to $165 a day, including mileage: *Avis* (phone: 830803 or 830004), *Dollar* (phone: 841709), *Econo-Rent* (phone: 841826), *Thrifty* (phone: 842699), and *Rentautos Kankun* (phone: 841175). On Cozumel, *Rentadora Cozumel* (phone: 21120) has jeeps — the best bet for local roads — for about $60 a day, including insurance, tax, and mileage. There are no rental agencies on Isla Mujeres.

MOPEDS Small motorbikes are an easy way to get around and are available at many Cancún hotels. The *Casa Maya* (phone: 830555) and *Frankie's* at the *Krystal* (phone: 831133) are two that rent mopeds for about $35 a day. On Cozumel, *Rentadora Cozumel* (phone: 21120 or 21503) charges $25 for a 24-hour rental. You can also rent mopeds at the *Plaza las Glorias* (phone: 22000) at the southern end of town. They also rent bicycles for $3 a day. On Isla Mujeres, motorbikes — available about 50 paces from the ferry dock, also for about $25 a day — are the only way to go.

TAXI Small green-and-white cabs are available at reasonable fares, according to zone, in Cancún City (fare from the city to the farthest hotel is about $12). Usually taxis are available at all the hotels on the island. If not, a doorman or bellman will call one quickly. In Cancún City there is a taxi stand on Avenida Tulum.

TOURS There are dozens of tour operators on Cancún, all of them with hotel offices on the island. Guests at smaller hotels can arrange for tours with any of these operators. Both bus and automobile tours are available.

WATER TAXI There are 15 daily passenger ferries to Isla Mujeres from Puerto Juárez, and 7 daily car ferries that leave from Punta Sam (between 7:15 AM and 10 PM). You can also take the passenger ferry to Cozumel from Playa del Carmen. Car ferries also leave from Puerto Morelos for Cozumel, but the wait is often quite long — with preference given to trucks and commercial transports. Another option is to hire a local fisherman to transport you; often members of the Fishing and Recreation Cooperative are willing to take passengers from one island to another for a reasonable fee.

SPECIAL EVENTS

Cozumel's annual *Carnival,* the island's version of *Mardi Gras,* takes place in February. Held in April or May, the annual *Regata del Sol al Sol,* organized by the *Isla Mujeres Yacht Club,* begins in St. Petersburg, Florida and finishes at Isla Mujeres. The annual spring *Amigos Regatta* — which circles Isla Mujeres — takes place after the *Regata del Sol al Sol.* In May, Cancún hosts an annual *International Jazz Festival.* The annual billfish tournament held on Cozumel each May brings in sportsmen from all over, especially Florida, which sends a virtual fleet. Very much worth seeing on the first day of spring or fall is the Chichén Itzá phenomenon, when light and shadow strike the Castillo Pyramid in such a manner that the snake god Kukulcán (also known as Quetzalcóatl) appears to be crawling down the side of the monument. The annual *Cancún Fair* takes place in November, with bullfights, cockfights, dances, and shows.

SHOPPING

In addition to such regional items as *guayabera* shirts (dressy-casual with a tucked — sometimes embroidered — front), *huipil* dresses, and Panama hats, goods and handicrafts from all over Mexico (and the world) are sold on Cancún. Besides native crafts, Cancún and Cozumel (both duty-free zones), have bargains on items produced outside the country. International discounted items include French perfume, Chinese silk, Cuban cigars, and tins of Danish butter. Locally designed sportswear and evening clothes are also good buys.

The big and bustling *Ki-Huic* (Av. Tulum near Cobá) is the city-sponsored crafts market, featuring some 44 stalls with an occasional find, but generally not the best prices in town. In the Hotel Zone, or Zona Turística, some of the most elegant shops can be found at *El Parián, Plaza Caracol, Mayfair, Kukulcán Plaza, La Mansión–Costa Blanca, Flamingo Plaza, Plaza Nautilus, Plaza Lagunas* and *Plaza Terramar* shopping centers. *El Zocalo,* a new outdoor shopping center in downtown Cancún, is another fun place to shop.

On Cozumel, the works of some 200 first-rate Mexican artists are displayed at *Bazar Cozumel* (Av. Juárez), which features silver tapestries with modern art motifs, weavings, pottery, and much more at fair prices. Also worth visiting is *Plaza del Sol,* a nest of nearly a dozen art, crafts, jewelry, and import boutiques, including *Los Cinco Soles,* which carries papier-mâché, carved wood, and onyx items.

In a place as tiny as Isla Mujeres, it's hard not to hit every stall or stand that has something of interest to sell. Unless you are looking for seashell necklaces or hand-dyed T-shirts, it's probably better to make the trek to Cancún, where the selection is bigger and the prices (although sometimes inflated by US standards) are better. The one major exception — *Rachat & Romé*'s beautifully crafted jewelry.

In many places, shoppers are expected to bargain for a purchase; to do this, a buyer really should know some basic Spanish, even if it's just a few numbers. Don't bargain in shops that have the sign *'precios fijos'* (fixed prices), in government shops (often called *Artes Populares*), or in hotel shops.

Shops on all three islands generally are open from 10 AM to 2 PM and from 4 to 7 PM; most major stores on Cancún stay open until 9 PM. Although stores post these hours, they may not always open on time.

CANCÚN

ARTLAND Rubbings, batiks, paintings, and jewelry, all inspired by Maya designs. Hotel Zone, *Flamingo Plaza* (phone: 832663).

CAROLI Jewelry and art objects crafted from sterling silver and semi-precious stones. Hotel Zone, *Flamingo Plaza* (phone: 850985).

LA CASITA Arts, crafts, decorative items, leather, jewelry, and Mexican-inspired clothing. Downtown, 115 Av. Tulum (phone: 841468).

LOS CASTILLO AND LILY CASTILLO Both are branches of one of Taxco's finest silversmith's, and both carry fine hand-crafted jewelry and art objects. Hotel Zone, *Plaza Caracol* (phone: 831084).

CHANTAL Select pieces of hand-crafted silver jewelry. The shop has a stunning African motif. Hotel Zone, *Plaza Caracol* (phone: 830450).

DON COTTON Wonderful T-shirts in vivid colors with rain forest, Caribbean, and Cancún motifs. The owners also run *Tango* (see below). Hotel Zone, *Plaza Caracol* (phone: 830114).

GALERÍAS COLONIAL Tableware with beautifully painted patterns, carved marble knickknacks, and chess sets. Hotel Zone, *Plaza Caracol* (phone: 830914).

GUCCI *Not* the real thing, it carries copies of the famous designer leather goods and shoes at very good prices. Hotel Zone, *Plaza Caracol* (phone: 832484) and *Plaza Flamingo* (phone: 851217).

LILI Fashionable swimwear and dresses. Hotel Zone, *Plaza Caracol* (phone: 833266).

ONYX AND HANDICRAFTS Good quality and prices for onyx pieces and other handicrafts. Hotel Zone, *Plaza Nautilus* (phone: 830699).

RONAY One of Mexico's most prestigious jewelers, specializing in gold designs. Hotel Zone, *Plaza Caracol* (phone: 831261).

SEBASTIAN The very finest in designer silver jewelry. Hotel Zone, *Plaza Caracol* (phone: 831815) and *Plaza Nautilus* (phone: 831949).

SYBELE High-quality imports from around the world, ranging from men's suits and women's lingerie to leather briefcases and fine perfume. Downtown at 109 Av. Tulum (phone: 841181) and *Plaza Carocol* (phone: 831738).

TANE Silver and vermeil jewelry, tableware, and art objects — many with traditional pre-Hispanic designs. Others are antique reproductions. In the *Camino Real* (phone: 830200) and *Hyatt Regency* (phone: 831349) hotels.

TANGO More of the same T-shirts that *Don Cotton* (see above) carries. In *Plaza Caracol* (phone: 830114).

XCARET An unusual and varied selection of some of the very best of Mexico's handicrafts — ceramics, textiles, papier-mâché — at reasonable prices. Hotel Zone, *Flamingo Plaza* (phone: 833256).

COZUMEL

LA CASITA The parent of the Cancún store and the source of more smashing Mexican resort clothes, as well as Sergio Bustamante's imaginative animal and bird sculptures. Av. Rafael E. Melgar (phone: 20198).

PAMA High-quality, duty-free imports — from jewelry and perfume to silk ties and ladies' fashions. 9 Av. Rafael E. Melgar (no phone).

PLAZA DEL SOL A nest of nearly a dozen art, crafts, jewelry, and import boutiques including *Orbi* (phone: 20685), purveyor of imported perfume, jewelry, and fancy foods; and *Los Cinco Soles* (no phone), for a good selection of handicrafts from throughout Mexico. Av. Rafael E. Melgar at Calle 8.

ISLA MUJERES

LA BAHÍA Near the ferry dock, this shop carries an upscale selection of beachwear, and rents diving gear (no phone).

RACHAT & ROMÉ Outstanding jewelry designed and crafted by the friendly Cuban who owns this place. In the flamingo-colored building just a few steps from the ferry dock. Corner of Av. Rueda Medina at Morelos (phone: 70250; fax: 70251).

BEACH (AND STREET) VENDORS Although "legally" outlawed in this part of Mexico, these ambulant salespeople still manage to materialize on almost every beach. They can be persistent, but unless you are interested in their wares, simply make your feelings understood with a firm "no."

SPORTS

On the islands, sports tend to be for participants, not spectators. The most convenient place to get the latest information is in the lobbies of most hotels.

BOATING Craft large and small, power and sail, crewed and uncrewed, are available on Cancún. Make arrangements at any hotel travel desk, or at *Marina Stouffer Presidente* (phone: 830200), *Club Lagoon* (phone: 831111), *Aqua Quin* (phone: 831883 or 830100), *Marina Camino Real* (phone: 830100), and *Royal Yacht Club* (phone: 850391). The *Regata del Sol al Sol* from St. Petersburg, Florida (held in April or May), ends at Isla Mujeres and is followed by the *Amigos* regatta around the island.

BULLFIGHTS Cancún has its own small bullring, which occasionally attracts major matadors. Corridas are held on Wednesdays at 3:30 PM at the *Plaza de Toros* in Cancún City. This modern 3-tiered arena has a seating capacity of 6,000, and provides ample parking.

FISHING The Mexican Caribbean coast offers some of the best deep-sea and fly fishing in the world, and American and European fishermen travel thousands of miles up and down the Yucatán coast to hook snook, bass, dorado, striped marlin, sailfish, red snapper, billfish, and shark.

Boats, both large and small, are available on Cancún at *Marina del Rey* (phone: 831748), *Club Lagoon* (phone: 831111), *Royal Yacht Club* (phone: 850391), and *Aqua Tours* (phone: 830227 or 830400). On Cozumel, try *Aquarius Travel* (2 Calle 3 Sur; phone: 21092) or *Cozumel Angler's Fleet*, 1 mile (1.6 km) south of town, at the *Club Nautico* (phone: 20118 or 21113) to charter boats. Here again, hotels can make all the arrangements. Firms charge about $65 per person per day or $240 to $310 for a half day for groups. On Isla Mujeres, *Cooperativa Transporte Turística* and *México Divers* (both at Av. Rueda Medina; phone: 70274) arrange trips for 4 for about $350 a day.

WHERE AND WHEN THEY BITE

Cancún is a haven for deep-sea and lagoon fishing. Sailfish and dolphin run from March to September; bluefin tuna in May; blue and white marlin in April and May; kingfish and wahoo from May through September. For information, go to the Chac-Mool pier or the *Playa Blanca* hotel pier.

The best fishing from Cozumel occurs from March to July for sailfish, bonito, and dolphin, and from May to September for wahoo and kingfish. Marlin, barracuda, and red snapper can also be found in the Caribbean here.

A casting-off spot for deep-sea fishermen, Isla Mujeres is most popular with anglers during the months of April and May, when the sailfish and marlin are biting. There are always plenty of boats available to take a paying customer to what locals hail as "the absolute best fishing spot in the Caribbean."

GOLF The area offers two claims to golfing fame.

TOP TEE-OFF SPOTS

Pok-Ta-Pok This 18-hole, par 72, Robert Trent Jones, Jr. course is renowned for its fast greens and wide fairways. *Pok-Ta-Pok* (Maya for stroke-by-stroke) is a very playable course with a sensational view of both the Caribbean Sea and the Nichupté Lagoon, but watch out for the ocean wind factor. The sand traps and water hazards are deadly, so most golfers carry about double their usual quota of balls. The course has a bar and restaurant, as well as putting greens. Golf clubs, shoes, and electric carts can be rented in the pro shop. The greens fee is $50; carts, $30. The club is open from 6 AM daily, but reservations are a near must. The pro is Felipe Galindo; the director, Gustavo Escalante (phone: 830871).

Puerto Aventuras This extraordinary 18-hole course was designed by Tommy Lehman, who incorporated natural cenotes (sinkholes) and ancient Maya ruins into the layout. With so many spectacular sights, it's tough to keep your eye on the ball. A tough par 72, the course is made especially challenging by its many sand traps, hazardous doglegs, and jungled roughs. Electric carts and clubs can be rented from the pro shop. The manager is Edgar H. Giffenig; the pro, Desiderio Coot. Km 269.5, Carretera Chetumal, Puerto Aventuras, Quintana Roo, Mexico (phone: 22211 or 22233).

Less daunting greens for less serious golfers include the *Oasis* hotel (phone: 850867), with its 9-hole course and the *Meliá Cancún* (phone: 851114), which has an 18-hole facility.

HORSEBACK RIDING *Rancho Loma Bonita* (phone: 840861 or 840907) has escorted horseback tours through the jungle, at 8 AM, 10:30 AM, and 1:30 PM, daily. Km 49 on Rte. 307, between Puerto Morelos and Playa del Carmen (phone: 840861 or 840907).

JET SKIING The lagoon is great for this water sport, which requires a minimum of learning time. The skis slow down and stay with you should you fall off. Available on Cancún at the *Royal Yacht Club* (phone: 850391) and *Aqua Ray* (phone: 833077).

SCUBA AND SNORKELING Mexico's Caribbean boasts some of the finest skin and scuba diving spots in the world. The clear, warm lagoons of Cancún, Cozumel, and Isla Mujeres teem with tropical fish, invertebrates, and incredible coral deposits of intricate formations and colorful hues. Palancar Reef, the second-largest coral atoll in the world and the largest in the Western hemisphere, is one of the most spectacular and popular dived regions in the world.

Several dive shops on Cozumel — including *Del Mar Aquatics* (in *La Ceiba;* phone: 20844), *Casa del Mar* (phone: 21900), *Dive House* (phone: 21953), *Aqua Safari* (phone: 20101), *Viajes y Deportes de Cozumel* (in the *Stouffer Presidente;* phone: 20322), *Neptuno Divers* (phone: 20999), *Big Blue* (phone: 20396), and the hotel dive shop at *Plaza las Glorias* (phone: 22000) offer rental equipment, instruction, and dive trips. Most hotels also offer diving facilities at somewhat higher rates, but the convenience is worth it. Scuba pool instruction (about 3 hours) costs about $50 per person. A 4- or 5-day seminar with a certified instructor that includes theory, shallow shore dives, a boat dive to a shallow reef, and a full boat dive to Palancar Reef is about $300 per person (less in the off-season). A full day's guided diving tour from Cozumel to Palancar, including equipment and lunch, is about $40. Equipment rentals run about $6 for a tank and weights; $6 to $12 for a regulator; $5 for fins, mask, and snorkel. Underwater camera rental is about $30 per day at *Cozumel Images* at the *Casa del Mar* hotel (phone: 21944).

BEST DEPTHS

Cancún is perfectly situated for swimming and diving amid coral reefs, fish, and turtles. The waters change color from turquoise to indigo to emerald to tourmaline. The best scuba diving and snorkeling place is in the waters off its southern point. Xcaret inlet, surrounded by jungle and the site of caverns and Maya ruins, is outstanding for skin diving (rental equipment available).

Isla Mujeres has transparent waters, coral reefs, and lagoons that are renowned among skin divers around the world. Ferries leave for the island from Puerto Juárez (on the mainland, just north of Cancún) 15 times daily (people and baggage only), and seven times daily from Punta Sam, just north of Puerto Juárez (people, cars, campers, and so on). The *Cooperativa Transporte Turística* (at Av. Rueda Medina; phone: 20274) rents boats and equipment. El Garrafón Beach, at the southern end of the 5-mile-long, half-mile-wide island, has crystal-clear waters and lovely coral gardens teeming with brightly colored, seemingly tame fish.

But it is Cozumel that takes the diving honors among scubaphiles. Just 11 miles off the Caribbean coast, this island is world-famous for its exquisitely clear water and its proximity to Palancar Reef, the second-largest reef in the world, where underwater visibility can be up to 250 feet. Diving is particularly good from May through August.

Chankanab Lagoon is another good spot — it swarms with reef fish. About one-quarter of a mile to the north and south of the lagoon, elkhorn coral and a variety of tropical fish are visible. Off the beach at *La Ceiba* hotel — probably the best equipped for divers — lies the hulk of a C-46 aircraft that "crashed" here in the movie *Cyclone.* Moonlight diving escapades through the fuselage of this wrecked plane, which settled amid clusters of coral, are a celebrated nocturnal event on the island.

Be aware that currents are strong on Cozumel. Don't dive without a guide.

SWIMMING AND SUNNING Though they are all beautiful, the beaches on Cancún's surf-pounded Caribbean side are narrower than those along the more serene Bahía de Mujeres and lagoon shores. The texture and whiteness of its sand are so distinctive that they inspired special studies by geologists, who found that many of the sand's individual grains contain microscopic, star-shape fossils of an organism called discoaster, extinct for 70 million years. Through the ages, the sea has ground and polished these grains till they've become brilliant and powder soft. What's more, their limestone composition has an air conditioning effect that makes the island's sand — even under the noonday sun — feel comfortable to bare feet or bodies in bikinis. Except right in Cancún City, chances are your hotel will have its own beach as well as a pool, but the master plan has provided several public strands as well.

In fact, Cancún boasts a 14-mile sandbar fringed with palms and gilded with plush hotels and a variety of recreational facilities. Primarily a spot for sports-minded pleasure seekers, many of Cancún's major hotels boast beaches. There are also more strands along Kukulcán Boulevard — the best is Chac-Mool, which has dressing rooms and showers available from 10 AM to 11 PM and a restaurant specializing in local seafood dishes.

DREAM BEACHES

Cozumel is edged by powder-white beaches, hidden coves, and azure-blue waters. The mainland side of the island has the more popular beaches, including San Francisco and San Juan. Beautiful, nearly deserted beaches can be found by following dirt paths on either side of the island. Chen Río Beach, on the southern end of the Caribbean side, is protected from unpredictable, turbulent Caribbean currents by a ledge of coral that juts into the sea. Punta Molas Beach, on the northern end of the island, is accessible by boat or jeep and offers a pleasant day's journey.

Isla Mujeres offers several white, uncrowded beaches. North Beach is the main one, covering the entire northern end of the island; the beach, on the Caribbean side, is good for sunbathing but dangerous for swimming. El Garrafón Beach, on the southern end of the island, is known for its crystal-clear waters and skin diving. The journey from the mainland (usually Cancún) to El Garrafón by boat is an adventure in itself — crew members catch fresh fish en route while passengers view schools of astonishingly "tame" tropical fish and turtles.

> **NOTE** Playa Tortuga is hands down the dirtiest, smelliest, most polluted beach in all Cancún. With so many nice beaches to choose from, why waste your time here?

TENNIS On Cancún there are courts at the *Aristos* (phone: 830011), *Calinda Cancún Beach* (phone: 831600), *Camino Real* (phone: 830100), *Cancún Sheraton* (phone: 831988), *Casa Maya* (phone: 830555), *Continental Villas Plaza* (phone: 831022), *Fiesta Americana Condesa* (phone: 851000), *Fiesta*

Americana Coral Beach (phone: 832900), *Hyatt Cancún Caribe* (phone: 830044), *Krystal Cancún* (phone: 831133), *Marriott Casa Magna* (phone: 852000), *Meliá Cancún* (phone: 851114), *Oasis* (phone: 850867), *Pok-Ta-Pok Golf Club* (phone: 830871), *Stouffer Presidente* (phone: 830200), and the *Villas Tacul* (phone: 830000). On Cozumel there are tennis courts at *La Ceiba* (phone: 20844), *Club Cozumel Caribe* (phone: 20100), the *Fiesta Americana Sol Caribe* (phone: 20466), the *Fiesta Inn* (phone: 22899), the *Holiday Inn* (phone: 22622), the *Meliá Mayan Cozumel* (phone: 20411), the *Stouffer Presidente Cozumel* (phone: 20322), and the *Villablanca* (phone: 20730). There are no courts available on Isla Mujeres.

WATER SKIING The lagoon behind the island of Cancún is the ideal place to learn or perfect this exhilarating sport. Make arrangements at any island hotel, at *Aqua Ray* (phone: 833007), *Marina del Rey* (phone: 831748), or at the *Club Lagoon* (phone: 831111). Boat time costs about $50 an hour.

WINDSURFING Once you've learned to stand on a surfboard, 2 or 3 hours of instruction are all you need. On Cancún lessons are available at several hotels, including the *Club Lagoon* (phone: 831111). Boards rent for about $10 an hour. Lessons cost $25, and several places offer weekly rates that include lessons. There are regattas Sundays at *Club Cancún*.

NIGHTCLUBS AND NIGHTLIFE

After-dark activity in Cancún City and the Hotel Zone has picked up considerably in the past few years. Reigning disco favorites are easily discernible by the crowds gathering outside before opening time (around 10 PM). Current hot spots are *Christine's* (at the *Krystal*); *La Boom* (on Kukulcán Blvd.); *Dady 'O* (near the *Convention Center*); and the *Hard Rock Café* (at *Plaza Lagunas*). *Note:* If ever a place lived up to its name, *Risky Business* (downtown on Av. Tulum) is it. Renowned for its high-decibel, deafening music that resembles a distorted brand of 1970s disco, its drinks are watered and its waiters have a nasty way of forgetting to bring you your change. *Carlos 'n' Charlie's Cancún* (on the marina) is a good place for food, drink, dancing, and meeting people; it's open until midnight. *Batachá Tropical,* a swinging disco, features live salsa music. *Daphny's* (at the *Cancún Sheraton*) is a popular video bar with live and taped music for dancing. *Sixties* (in the *Marriott*) plays dance music from the 1950s, 1960s, and 1970s. The *Camino Real* offers a nightly cabaret of Cuban music and dance. And don't forget to try the world-famous hurricane cocktail (served in a 24-ounce glass) at *Pat O'Brien's Bar* (on Kukulcán Blvd. across from the *Flamingo* hotel).

For lots of silly fun, there's the Pirate's Night Adventure cruise, available on both Cancún and Cozumel; for more information call the tourist office (phone: 843238). Not to be missed is the *Ballet Folklórico* at the *Continental Villas Plaza* hotel presented nightly at 7 PM,. Tickets include dinner and open bar (phone: 831022). A torchlit beach, a delicious buffet, and exotic drinks make for a romantic evening at the *Hyatt Cancún Caribe*'s Mexican Night, Mondays, Wednesdays, Fridays, and Saturdays at 7 PM. The *Sheraton* hosts a similar event on Wednesdays at 7:30 PM, and *Plaza las Glorias* hosts one on Tuesdays.

On Cozumel, *Scaramouche* (downtown) is lively and attempts sophistication. *Neptuno* (next to *El Acuario* restaurant on the *malecón*) is also popular. No matter where you go, the crowds tend to be young.

On Isla Mujeres, there are *Buho's Disco Bar, Calypso, Tequila Video Disco,* and *Casablanca,* as well as beach parties and night cruises.

A SOBERING THOUGHT Also known as "muppet," *coscorrón* is a concoction of half tequila, half Sprite, blended in a covered shot glass by a couple of strong raps on the imbiber's table or head (depending on how many he or she has had already). It's the quickest route to a Mexican hangover. Usually offered as a come-on to attract *turistas,* the *coscorrón* — literally head-knocker — is almost always produced with the lowest-grade tequila on the market. No self-respecting *Mexicano* would fall for it. If you want to try tequila, do it in style, with a slice of lime and a lick of salt, and make sure you choose a decent brand name such as Sauza; Commemorativo is an especially good type of Sauza tequila.

LOW LEVEL OF TOLERANCE Nearly every city in Mexico — with the exception of Mexico City — has a Zona de Tolerancia: Cancún's "zone of tolerance," or red-light district, is just north of the city, and it's a very enterprising place. The most obvious deterrent for sampling the wares of the ladies of the evening these days is the threat of AIDS and other social diseases. If this is not enough of a deterrent, consider the fact that many of these charming young girls are in fact charming young men in drag, and their main objective is to liberate a visitor of cash and valuables.

Best in Town

CHECKING IN

All the hotels on Cancún are relatively new (some are newer than others), aspire to be lavish, and boast some of the highest prices in Mexico. Travelers on a budget, however, can find less costly accommodations away from the major beaches. During high season (December to May), expect to pay $180 to $270 per day for a double room in those places we call very expensive (the highest price would be for a 2-bedroom villa); $110 to $175 in expensive places; $75 to $100, moderate; and $60 or less, inexpensive.

Prices drop as much as 50% during the summer months. Even with close to 20,000 hotel rooms, Cancún really does not have enough hotel space to meet the demand during the winter months, so it is best to go only with a confirmed reservation.

The more luxurious Cozumel hotels are in either the North Zone or the South Zone, above and below the town. The in-town hotels (most have neither beach nor pool) appeal most to budget travelers. Hotel prices on Cozumel are similar to those on Cancún, and it is also best to arrive here with a prepaid reservation. Hotel rates on Isla Mujeres tend to be moderate to inexpensive. All telephone numbers on Cancún are in the 98 area code, on Cozumel and on Isla Mujeres 987, unless otherwise indicated.

NOTE Parking can be a problem at some hotels.

MOTELS NO! There is a very different connotation given to the word *motel* in Mexico. While a Mexican *hotel* is generally comparable to the US version, a *motel* is a whole other story; it serves one purpose, and that is to rent by the hour. These *auto-hoteles*, as they are also advertised, have curtained garages to insure the privacy of any "guests" who might not like their license plates seen. Many an unsuspecting tourist and his family have pulled into a *motel* hoping to enjoy a relaxing evening, only to discover that there is no furniture (other than one rather predominant bed), no closet, and no phone in the room.

For an unforgettable Mexico vacation experience, we begin with our favorites, followed by our recommendations of cost and quality choices of hotels, listed by place and price category.

ROOMS AT THE TOP
CANCÚN

Camino Real Located at the northeast tip of Cancún, this pleasure palace has 381 air conditioned rooms situated in two beautiful buildings, both offering magnificent views of the Caribbean. The older, main building (designed by architect Ricardo Legoretta) reflects the Maya culture. The newer *Royal Beach Club* offers 67 deluxe guest rooms and 18 suites featuring additional amenities such as concierge service, complimentary continental breakfast, and afternoon tea. All rooms have balconies, and are decorated in a colorful Mexican design. Also, a freshwater pool with a swim-up bar, a saltwater lagoon, 3 restaurants, tennis courts, and plenty of water sports make this hotel one of the best around. On the island (phone: 830100; 800-228-3000 in the US; fax: 831730).

Continental Villas Plaza Popular among kings, presidents, and movie stars, these 638 Mediterranean villas are currently considered the poshest address in Cancún. With 7 restaurants from which to choose, guests can sample a different cuisine every night during a week's stay. There are also 2 tennis courts, 3 swimming pools, and a squash court, plus a private marina. The crystalline beach is some of the prettiest oceanfront property on the island. Most rooms have a majestic view of the Caribbean and many also boast a private balcony with Jacuzzi. On the island. Km 11 on Kukulcán Blvd. (phone: 831022 or 851444; 800-88-CONTI in the US).

Fiesta Americana Coral Beach Designed in Mediterranean style with a definite calypso accent, this super-luxury, massive flamingo-pink complex is considered by many to be a true Mexican masterpiece. And though it may be a bit too rococo for some gringo tastes, it's where all of Cancún's elite hold their social events. A self-contained beachside wonderland, it offers deluxe suites, restaurants, bars, a swimming pool, tennis courts, satellite TV, and its own gym. On the island (phone: 832900; 800-FIESTA-1 in the US).

Hyatt Cancún Caribe Those who like all the comforts of home, but with an elegant, modern touch, select this hillside paradise as their base in Cancún. The grounds seem to go on forever, with serried terraces, gardens, and verandahs giving an air of spaciousness — and offering spectacular views. Located close to all the best shopping as well as one of the choicest strips of beach on the island, this elegant 200-unit resort boasts several restaurants — including the *Blue Bayou,* specializing in superb Cajun cooking. Tennis courts, 3 swimming pools, and a Jacuzzi are an enticement to work off the extra calories. On the island. Km 8.5 on Kukulcán Blvd. (phone: 830044; 800-233-1234 in the US).

COZUMEL

Club Cozumel Caribe Off the beaten path and surrounded by gardens that would make Scarlett O'Hara forget Tara, this spacious, air conditioned, 260-room resort is the height of elegance in Cozumel. That's the good news. The bad news is that it's so far removed from everything else on the island that you may have trouble getting a taxi to and from snorkeling at Palancar Reef or shopping in San Miguel. But then, when in paradise, why hurry to leave? Also offered here are satellite TV, a restaurant, a bar, a swimming pool, and tennis courts. (phone: 20100; 800-327-2254 in the US).

Plaza Las Glorias The only luxury hotel in town that is on the beach, this is a favorite haunt for return visitors. Each of the 170 suites has an ocean view and a private balcony. There are 2 restaurants, a lobby bar with live music, and an oversize pool. But the main focus of action is the dive shop, manned by certified *PADI* (*Professional Association of Diving Instructors*) personnel. The sea around the hotel is an ideal spot for first-time divers; sunken cannon, coral reef, and abundant schools of tropical fish are there for the viewing. This is also one of the few places in the entire Yucatán that has facilities for the handicapped. South Zone (phone: 22000; 800-342-AMIGO in the US).

ISLA MUJERES

Cristalmar Tucked away on the inward coast, this new 38-suite property has 1-, 2-, and 3-bedroom deluxe units with air conditioning and satellite TV. The property also boasts its own secluded beach, an excellent dive shop, and the nicest pool in town. Lote 16, Fraccionamiento Paraiso Laguna (phone: 800-441-0472 in the US; at press time, the hotel did not have a local direct line).

CANCÚN

VERY EXPENSIVE

Fiesta Americana Its appearance is unique, with a Mexican pink façade and a fountain-filled lobby. Each of the 280 rooms has rattan furnishings and a balcony overlooking the water. The pool area is very nicely laid out with thatch-roofed, open-air restaurant and bars, beyond which is the aqua blue bay. Snorkeling gear is available poolside. The lobby is a pretty place for before-dinner cocktails, with a strolling mariachi band. On the island (phone: 831400; 800-FIESTA-1 in the US; fax: 832502).

Fiesta Americana Condesa A Grand Tourism hotel (Mexico's five-star rating), it has three towers, each with its own atrium lounge covered by a glass, *palapa*-shape roof. The decor is mostly rattan complemented by fresh, vivid colors. There are 500 rooms — including 27 suites with Jacuzzis on private terraces — plus a split-level pool with a 66-foot waterfall, 5 restaurants, 3 lighted tennis courts (all indoor and air conditioned), a jogging track, a spa, a small beach, and a lobby bar where live music is played in the evenings. Kukulcán Blvd. (phone: 851000; 800-FIESTA-1 in the US; fax: 851800).

Hyatt Regency Beautifully housed under a glass atrium, this hotel has 300 rooms, all with ocean views. It has a pool, 3 bars, and 3 restaurants (see *Scampi* in *Eating Out*). On the island (phone: 830966, 800-233-1234 in the US; fax: 831349).

Krystal Cancún With lush, thick greenery outside and in, it offers 270 rooms and suites, tennis, and 5 fine restaurants (see *Bogart's* in *Eating Out*), including a good breakfast buffet. On the island (phone: 831133; 800-213-9860 in the US; fax: 831790).

Marriott Casa Magna A 6-story hostelry of contemporary design, it is stunningly decorated with Mexican textures and colors. All rooms have balconies providing a view of either the Caribbean or the lagoon. Four restaurants — including a Japanese steakhouse — nightclub, pool, Jacuzzi, and 2 lighted tennis courts. Hotel Zone (phone: 852000; 800-228-9290 in the US; fax: 851731).

Meliá Cancún With a waterfall that cascades over part of its entrance, this 450-unit marble and glass complex has a huge, central atrium that looks and, unfortunately, *feels* like a tropical jungle. It's all beautifully decorated with bright tiles, bentwood, and wicker. Four restaurants, 5 bars, 3 tennis courts, and a small, par 54, 18-hole golf course. Hotel Zone (phone: 851114; 800-336-3542 in the US; fax: 851085).

Meliá Turquesa A giant white pyramid that slopes down to the beach, it offers 446 rooms decorated in soft colors and equipped with satellite TV, mini-bars, and safe-deposit boxes. Two restaurants, 3 bars, a coffee shop, pool, and 2 lighted tennis courts. Hotel Zone (phone: 832544; 800-336-3542 in the US; fax: 851241).

Oasis Built in the tradition of an ancient Maya city, this 1,000-room complex of angled structures offers 7 restaurants, 9 bars, satellite TV, and the longest swimming pool (nearly a third of a mile) in the Caribbean, plus 4 tennis courts and a 9-hole golf course. The only problem is that it is far from town. Km 47 on Kukulcán Blvd. (phone: 850867; 800-44-OASIS in the US; fax: 850131).

Radisson Sierra Plaza The 261 rooms are elegantly appointed, with a Southwestern flair. All guestrooms are air conditioned and have color TV sets, colorful furnishings, and tile floors. The oceanfront property features 2 restaurants, 3 lounges, 2 snack bars, an outdoor pool, a fitness center, 2 tennis courts, and plenty of water sports. Hotel Zone (phone: 832444; 800-333-3333 in the US; fax: 833486).

Ritz-Carlton Cancún Opened early last year, this super-luxury resort features 370 guestrooms, including 52 executive suites, and 2 Presidential suites. All rooms are air conditioned and offer private balconies with sea views, mini-bars, 2 bathrooms and remote-control TV sets. On premises: a health club, 2 swimming pools, and 3 lighted tennis courts, as well as 3 restaurants. Kukulcán Blvd. (phone: 851212; 305-446-0776 in Florida; 800-241-3333 elsewhere in the US).

Stouffer Presidente On the golf links and boasting 1 tennis court, fishing, and water skiing, this stately, 295-room hostelry is a favorite of sports enthusiasts. Its beach and location are among the best on Cancún. On the island (phone: 830200, 830414, or 830202; 800-HOTELS-1 in the US; fax: 832515).

Villas Tacul A colony of 23 Spanish-style villas with gardens, patios, and kitchens. With 2 to 5 bedrooms per house, on a narrow but pleasant beach; also offers 2 tennis courts. Good for families and congenial 2- or 3-couple groups. Km 5.5 on Kukulcán Blvd. (phone: 830000; 800-842-0193 in the US; fax: 830349).

EXPENSIVE

Calinda Beach Cancún Situated on the best beach on the island, between the Nichupté Lagoon and Bahía Mujeres, this hostelry isn't as lavish as many of its neighbors; very popular, it boasts a loyal following of return guests. All 460 rooms have ocean views. Facilities include a restaurant, bars, a pool, tennis, and a gym (phone: 831600; 800-228-5151 in the US; fax: 831857).

Casa Maya Originally built as condominiums, the 350 rooms and suites here are large, to say the least, with immense walk-in closets, sinks the size of bathtubs, and tubs the size of swimming pools. Among the amenities are moped rentals, 2 lighted tennis courts, a swimming pool, a restaurant, and cordial service. The place seems to be especially popular with families. On the island (phone: 830555; 800-44-UTELL in the US; fax: 831188).

Club Med Boasting one of the widest beaches on the island, it's one of the prime places to stay on Cancún. The 410 rooms, each with 2 European single beds and traditional Mexican decor, are set in 3-story bungalows facing either the ocean or the lagoon. Windsurfing, sailing, snorkeling, and scuba diving (including scuba instruction) are included in the basic rate, as are all meals. Lunch and dinner include complimentary wine. There's entertainment nightly. At Punta Nizuc (phone: 842090; 800-CLUB-MED in the US).

Omni All of the 334 rooms have large terraces; there are also 35 suites and 27 villas. Facilities include 2 lighted tennis courts, 8 restaurants, bars, a gameroom, and a health center. Not much of a beach, but hammocks have been strung up on the grounds for lounging and sipping tropical drinks by the sea. Four of the rooms are specially equipped for disabled guests, and there are access ramps to all public areas. Km 16.5 on Kukulcán Blvd. (phone: 850714; 800-THE-OMNI in the US; fax: 850184).

Royal Solaris A Maya pyramid–like structure, it has 280 rooms (including 13 junior suites), an Olympic-size pool, pleasant beach, health club, and social programs. Km 23 on Kukulcán Blvd. (phone: 850100; 800-368-9779 in the US; fax: 850354).

Sheraton Resort This 748-room self-contained gem is set apart on its own beach, which it shares with a small Maya temple. Facilities include 6 tennis courts, 6 pools, and *Daphny's* video bar with live music; there are also aerobics classes and scuba lessons. On the island (phone: 831988; 800-325-3535 in the US; fax: 850202).

Westin Regina This resort complex features 385 rooms, each with an ocean or lagoon view; the 94 tower rooms have private balconies (as do some in the low-rise building). Facilities include 5 outdoor pools, 2 lighted tennis courts, a health club and recreation center, a water sports center, and a boat dock for access to evening cruises and water sports. There are also 2 restaurants and 2 lounges. Kukulcán Blvd., at Punta Nizuc (phone: 850086; 800-228-3000 in the US; fax: 850296).

MODERATE

América There are 180 large rooms, each with its own terrace, at this pleasant place. It is not right on the beach, but does provide free shuttle service to its own beach club. There's a pool, restaurant, bar, and coffee shop. Av. Tulum (phone: 847500; fax: 841953).

Aristos The friendly scale and Mexican hospitality make for easy comfort here. There are 244 smallish but pleasant rooms. Inviting pool area, beach, 2 lighted tennis courts, and restaurant. Km 9.5 on Kukulcán Blvd. (phone: 830011; 800-5-ARISTOS in the US; fax: 830078).

Club Lagoon This secluded collection of 89 adobe-type dwellings on quiet Laguna Nichupté, including rooms and 2-level suites, is a real find. One picturesque courtyard opens onto another, with flowers playing colorfully against the white cottages; the best face the lagoon. It also has 2 restaurants, 2 bars, and a nautical center. On the island (phone: 831111; fax: 831808).

Fiesta Inn Golf Cancún Decorated in shades of soft pastels, the 120 rooms here are set right at the edge of the *Pok-Ta-Pok* golf course. Guests receive a 50% discount on greens fees, and they are allowed use of the facilities and services of other Fiesta Americana hotels on the island (charges are automatically billed to rooms). There is no beach, but free transportation is provided to the hotel's beach club. On the island (phone: 832200; 800-FIESTA-1 in the US; fax: 832532).

Playa Blanca A pioneer among Cancún's hotels (it opened in 1974), this link in the Best Western chain has a small beachfront, 161 rooms, a pool, and every water sport imaginable. Since it's next door to the marina, the boating facilities are excellent. On the island (phone: 830344; 800-221-4726 in the US; fax: 830904).

INEXPENSIVE

Plaza Caribe A good bet downtown, across from the bus station. The air conditioned rooms fill up fast. Cancún City (phone: 841377; fax: 846352).

Plaza del Sol Half-moon–shape, with two stylized canoes over its portals, it has 87 rooms, a pool, restaurant, bar, and free transportation to the beach. Cancún City (phone: 843888; fax: 844393).

COZUMEL

EXPENSIVE

Coral Princess Club Set on the north end of the island, this posh new resort offers 70 units, each with kitchenette and private terrace. There's also a pool, a restaurant, and a video bar (phone: 23200 or 23323; 800-272-3243 in the US; fax: 20016).

El Cozumeleño This property has 80 large rooms, 3 restaurants, a bar, a tennis court, and a free-form pool. Santa Pilar (phone: 20050; 800-437-3923 in the US; fax: 20381).

Fiesta Americana Sol Caribe A beautiful 322-room resort 'twixt beach and jungle, it has 3 tennis courts, good diving facilities, and a fine dining room. South Zone (phone: 20466; 800-FIESTA-1 in the US; fax: 21301).

Holiday Inn Cozumel Reef One of the newer high-quality accommodations on the island, this 165-room inn has 3 restaurants, 2 bars, 2 lighted tennis courts, a health spa, and a private boat dock. South Zone (phone: 22622; 800-465-4329 in the US; fax: 22666).

Meliá Mayan Cozumel Set on the isolated north end of the coast, this 12-story high-rise on the beach has 200 rooms and suites, an abundance of terraces, 2 tennis courts, a *Fiesta Mexicana* on Thursdays, and a *Caribbean Fiesta* on Fridays. Playa Santa Pilar (phone: 20411; 800-336-3542 in the US; fax: 21599).

Stouffer Presidente Cozumel The original luxury establishment on the island and still one of the best, it has 253 rooms, a pleasant beach, nice pool, tennis, and an excellent dining room. South Zone (phone: 20322; 800-HOTELS-1 in the US; fax: 21360).

MODERATE

Barracuda Near the shopping area, this 51-unit place has in-room bars. No pool. Rate includes continental breakfast, served on the beach. Av. Rafael E. Melgar, south of town (phone: 20002; fax: 20884).

La Ceiba Well equipped and conveniently located for scuba divers, this 115-room hostelry has satellite TV, spa, tennis, a restaurant, and lounge. Paradise Point (phone: 20844; 800-777-5873 in the US; fax: 20065).

Club Cantarell Situated 1½ miles (2 km) from town, this beachfront property offers 81 small but pleasant rooms and 16 suites, all recently remodeled. Facilities include 2 pools, a Jacuzzi, a restaurant, and scooter and car rentals. North Zone (phone: 20144; 800-272-3243 in the US; fax: 20016).

Fiesta Inn Part of the Fiesta chain, the 3-story, colonial-style hostelry is surrounded by beautiful gardens and connected to the beach by a tunnel. The

178 rooms and 2 suites have satellite TV. Facilities include a large pool, tennis court, motorcycle rental, dive shop, restaurant, bar, and coffee shop. Km 1.7 Costera Sur (phone: 22899; 800-FIESTA-1 in the US; fax: 22154).

Mara Most of the 48 rooms face the lovely beach. There's also a pleasant pool, a restaurant, and a dive shop. North Zone (phone: 20300; 800-221-6509 in the US; fax: 20105).

La Perla Right on the beach, this 4-story, 22-room hotel has its own swimming cove and a pier with diesel, light, and water connections for private yachts. Also a pool, deli-bar, dive packages, and a quiet, comfortable, unpretentious atmosphere. 2 Av. Francisco I. Madero, PO Box 309 (phone: 20188; 800-852-6404 in the US; fax: 22611).

Playa Azul A family favorite, this member of the Best Western group offers 60 rooms and suites, a restaurant, bar, and water sports. North of San Miguel, at Km 4 on Carr. San Juan (phone: 20033; 800-528-1234 in the US; fax: 20110).

Sol Cabañas del Caribe Informal and friendly, this semitropical hideaway on one of the island's best beaches has 50 rooms, a small pool, and 9 cabañas. North Zone (phone: 20017 or 20072; 800-336-3542 in the US; fax: 21599).

INEXPENSIVE

Villablanca Though its facilities resemble those of a resort hotel — tennis court, pool, dive shop, boat for up to 60 divers, classes in all water sports — this property has only 50 rooms and suites, some with Jacuzzis and all with air conditioning and fans. Across the street, on the water's edge, is *Amadeus,* its restaurant-bar–beach club. Playa Paraíso at Km 2.9 (phone: 20730 or 20865).

ISLA MUJERES

MODERATE

Cabañas María del Mar At the north end of the island, it has 48 units (including 10 cabañas), a restaurant, and a full-service 20-slip marina. The proprietors, the Limas, make everyone feel at home. Av. Carlos Lazo (phone: 70179; fax: 70156).

Perla del Caribe This 3-story hotel offers 90 rooms, all with balconies. There is also a restaurant and pool. 2 Av. Madero (phone: 70444; 800-258-6454 in the US; fax: 70011).

INEXPENSIVE

Berny A downtown hostelry with 40 rooms, a spacious lobby, a pool, and a restaurant. Av. Juárez (phone: 70025; fax: 70026). Inexpensive.

Posada del Mar This pleasant 42-room hostelry is one of the best on the island, with palm-shaded grounds, a fine restaurant (see *Eating Out*), bar, pool, laundromat, and air conditioning. Across from the beach. 15 Av. Rueda Medina (phone: 70300 or 70044; fax: 70266).

Roca Mar Thirty-four basic but pleasant rooms, all with a view. There is also a restaurant. Av. Nicolás Bravo y Guerrero (phone: 70101).

EATING OUT

Hotel food on Cancún is better than average, because the hotelleis want to keep the money spent on food in the house, which means that the non-hotel restaurants must work extra hard to lure customers. There is a sampling of ethnic cooking, and by all means try Yucatecan specialties, which are quite different from standard Mexican fare. Start the day with eggs *moltuleños* — fried eggs on a tortilla — black beans, and a spicy sauce. And don't miss delicious and filling Yucatán lime soup, which also contains chicken, vegetables, and tortillas.

Almost all the restaurants on Cozumel are in town, although a few, open only for lunch, are out on the beaches. Restaurant prices on Cozumel and Isla Mujeres are somewhat more moderate than those on Cancún.

Expect to pay $40 to $60 for two in restaurants we list as expensive; about $30 at moderate places; and $20 in inexpensive ones. Prices do not include wine, tips, or drinks. All restaurants listed below accept Master-Card and Visa; a few also accept American Express and Diners Club. Unless noted otherwise, restaurants listed below are open daily. All telephone numbers on Cancún are in the 98 area code, on Cozumel and on Isla Mujeres 987, unless otherwise indicated.

CANCÚN

EXPENSIVE

Augustus Caesar Seafood and traditional Italian dishes are served with flair in pretty surroundings. Live music is featured from 8:30 PM to midnight. No shorts or T-shirts. Reservations advised. At *La Mansión–Costa Blanca Shopping Center* (phone: 833384).

Blue Bayou Cajun and creole fare and specialty drinks are served in a multilevel dining area suspended among waterfalls and lush tropical greenery. Live jazz. Dinner only. Reservations necessary. *Hyatt Cancún Caribe* (phone: 830044, ext. 54).

Bogart's International dishes served with quiet elegance in exotic Moroccan surroundings. Seatings at 7 and 9:30 PM. No shorts or T-shirts. Reservations advised. At the *Krystal Cancún* (phone: 831133).

Calypso The decor of this dining spot combines elegance and a tropical exuberance, with fountains, pools, and live reggae music to enhance the romantic seaside ambience. The menu features first-rate Caribbean fare, with a strong emphasis on seafood — try the braised fish with lobster medallions and scallion sauce. Dinner only. Reservations advised. Hotel Zone, *Camino Real* hotel (phone: 830100, ext. 8060).

Carlos 'n' Charlie's Fun 'n' games are the strong points at this branch of Mexico's well-known restaurant chain, where good spareribs and shrimp are served. There's also a small dockside disco where diners can dance the night away. No reservations. On the island (phone: 830846).

La Dolce Vita Modern decor is the backdrop to intimate dining, where the sweet life is manifested in tasty pasta and seafood dishes. Dinner only. Reservations advised. 87 Cobá, in Cancún City (phone: 841384).

Grimond's Formerly the mayor's home, this elegant dining place has European furniture, Oriental rugs, English china, and French crystal — not to mention 4 sitting rooms, 1 dining room, and an upstairs piano bar. The French chef recommends shrimp sautéed in cherry wine sauce. Jackets are not required; shorts and sandals are not permitted. Dinner only. Reservations advised. On the island (phone: 830438).

Gypsy's A touch of Spain in the Mexican Caribbean, this rustic-looking eatery specializes in Iberian cooking (the paella is exceptional). Flamenco dancers entertain nightly. Open for dinner only. No reservations. On the Nichupté Lagoon, across from the *Villas Plaza* hotel (phone: 832015 or 832120).

La Habichuela Set in an authentically reproduced Maya garden complete with miniature ruins, this is the place local folk book for a night out and for *mar y tierra,* alias surf and turf. Reservations advised. 25 Margaritas, in Cancún City (phone: 843158).

Hacienda el Mortero An authentic copy of a Mexican hacienda in Súchil, Durango, it specializes in steaks and Mexican haute cuisine. Reservations advised. In the *Krystal Cancún,* Km 9 on Kukulcán Blvd. (phone: 831133).

Iguana Wana This trendy spot — which bills itself as "a contemporary Mexican café and bar" — offers live jazz and a varied menu including Tex-Mex chili and buckets of peel-your-own shrimp. No reservations. *Plaza Caracol Shopping Center* (phone: 830829).

Jaguari's This is the place to sink your teeth into a thick, juicy steak. Run by a Brazilian, it offers premium beef cuts served with a South American *churrasquería* sauce. Reservations advised. On Gaviota Azul Beach (phone: 832939).

Lorenzillo's Set under a giant *palapa* that extends over Nichupté Lagoon, this seafood restaurant specializes in soft-shell shrimp and rock lobster. Open daily from 10 AM to 11:30 PM. Casual dress okay, but no shorts or T-shirts. Reservations unnecessary. Hotel Zone (phone: 831254).

El Pescador Perhaps the best seafood eatery in Cancún, it serves fresh lobster, shrimp, and red snapper on Mexican pottery. Don't miss the Yucatecan lime soup or the hot rolls, and try for a table outside, on the fan-cooled terrace. Closed Mondays. Reservations unnecessary. 28 Tulipanes, in Cancún City (phone: 842673).

Scampi Superb northern Italian fare — delicious pasta, meat, and seafood — is served in a beautiful setting. The service is impeccable. *Hyatt Regency* (phone: 830966).

Señor Frog's Under the same ownership as *Carlos 'n' Charlie's,* it offers a similar menu (see above). Open for breakfast, lunch, and dinner. At Km 5.5 on Kukulcán Blvd. (phone: 832931).

Seryna Japanese specialties such as sushi, teppanyaki, sukiyaki, yosenabe, shabu-shabu, tempura, and other traditional dishes are served in a pretty setting. Reservations advised. *Flamingo Plaza Shopping Center* (phone: 851155 or 832995).

MODERATE

Bombay Bicycle Club Casual and comfortable, this spot offers fare from the States — good hamburgers, barbecued ribs, and calorie-filled desserts. Excellent, friendly service. Open 7 AM to 11 PM. No reservations. Kukulcán Blvd., across from Playa Tortuga (no phone).

Jalapeños A nonstop fiesta atmosphere with live reggae music nightly. Mexican and seafood items are the specialties of the house. No reservations. *La Hacienda Shopping Center* (phone: 832896 or 832682).

Johnny Rockets Rock 'n' roll with a 1950s theme attracts visitors to this hamburger eatery–video bar. The music is hot, and the food even hotter. Definitely not a place for easy listening. No reservations. *Plaza Terramar Shopping Center* (phone: 833092).

La Mamá de Tarzan Another link in the ubiquitous Anderson's chain, this one is a cafeteria-style eatery with good salad, a lively bar, nightly fiesta, and dancing on the pier. Reservations advised. Opposite Chac-Mool Beach (phone: 831092).

Pizza Rolandi All kinds of Italian dishes are served in an informal, outdoor setting. Reservations unnecessary. 12 Av. Cobá, Cancún City (phone: 844047).

Torremolinos Paella, crayfish, and crab done the Spanish way. No reservations. Tulum and Xcaret (phone: 843639).

Los Almendros Authentic Yucatecan food and the same management as its famous Mérida namesake. Reservations unnecessary. Av. Bonampak and Sayíl, Cancún City (phone: 840807).

Café Amsterdam Reasonably priced European dishes are served in this intimate bistro. The delicious bread is baked on the premises, and there is a huge salad and fresh fruit bar. Open daily, except Mondays, from 7 AM to 11 PM. Reservations unnecessary. 70 Av. Yaxchilán (phone: 844098).

100% Natural The place to go for fresh fruit drinks, salads, sandwiches, and fruit and vegetable platters. Live jazz music nightly. No reservations. 6 Sunyaxchen (phone: 843617). *Terramar Shopping Center* in the Hotel Zone (phone: 831180) .

COZUMEL

EXPENSIVE

Acuario Once a real aquarium, it's now an elegant seafood restaurant, with entertainment provided by an immense tankful of exotic tropical fish in the middle of the room. Reservations advised. On the *malecón* (phone: 21097).

Carlos 'n' Charlie's and Jimmy's Kitchen The Cozumel branch of Mexico's favorite restaurant chain, where people come for ribs and good times. Reservations advised. On the *malecón* (phone: 20191).

Donatello A premier Italian dining place with a New Orleans French Quarter ambience, it serves superb fresh pasta and offers a beautiful ocean view. Open daily for dinner only. Reservations advised. 131 Av. Melgar Sur (phone: 22586 or 20090).

Morgan's Lobster thermidor and special coffees are favorites at this very comfortable, popular wood cabin serving good steaks and seafood on the main plaza. Reservations advised (phone: 20584).

Pepe's Grill This romantic spot by the waterfront has excellent seafood and steaks. A variety of live music is featured nightly. Reservations advised. Av. Rafael E. Melgar (phone: 20213).

MODERATE

Casa Denis The menu varies at this cozy eatery, where Yucatecan dishes are served under a tropical fruit tree. Reservations advised. Just off the south side of the main square in San Miguel (phone: 20067).

Mezcalito's Set on the surf-pounded Caribbean side of the island, this large open-air *palapa* serves up some of the tastiest grilled shrimp and fish on the island. The atmosphere — white sand, ocean breezes, and friendly chatter — is unbeatable. A good spot, too, just to stop for a cold beer or a piña colada. No reservations. Punta Morena (no phone).

Las Palmeras Just opposite the ferry dock, it's a great meeting place offering a varied menu for every meal. The homemade biscuits and French toast are a treat. Reservations unnecessary. On the *malecón* (phone: 20532).

Pancho's Backyard The food is just what you would expect — good and plenty — served on hand-crafted ceramic pottery. Strolling mariachis give this place a certain *sabor mexicano.* No reservations. On the waterfront at 8th St. (phone: 22142).

Plaza Leza A sidewalk café serving good Mexican snacks, charcoal-broiled steaks, and seafood. Reservations advised. On the main plaza (phone: 21041).

INEXPENSIVE

San Francisco The fare is — what else? — seafood (try the snail ceviche), and a band plays in the afternoons. Open daily for lunch only. Reservations unnecessary. A quarter mile from San Francisco Beach and about 9 miles (14 km) from town (no phone).

Sports Page If you can't survive without the *Super Bowl* or the *World Series,* stop in and watch the games on TV while munching on a burger and fries. No reservations. Av. 5 (no phone).

Las Tortugas Simple but good sandwiches are served here, along with good, cold beer. Don't be put off by the nondescript surroundings. Reservations unnecessary. 82 Av. 10 Norte, in the heart of town (no phone).

ISLA MUJERES

EXPENSIVE

Ciro's Lobster House A wide selection of Mexican wines accompanies the lobster and red snapper served here. Reservations advised. 11 Matamoros, in town (phone: 70102).

MODERATE

Gomar Lobster and fresh fish are best enjoyed on the romantic terrace, where tables sport bright, striped Mexican cloths during the day, white at night. You can also dine indoors. Reservations unnecessary. Hidalgo and Madero (phone: 70142).

Hacienda Gomar Known for its good seafood buffet and exotic drinks. On the west side of the island on the road to El Garrafón (no phone).

Los Pájaros Facing the beach on the north end of town, this *palapa*-style eatery serves good Mexican fare. Reservations unnecessary. *Posada del Mar* hotel (phone: 70044).

Buho's Paradise Great for late snacks. Reservations unnecessary. Next to *Cabañas María del Mar* (phone: 70179).

Pizza Rolandi Pizza cooked in a wood-burning oven, and other Italian dishes. Reservations unnecessary. Hidalgo between Madero and Abasolo (phone: 70430).

BEWARE: MOBILE FOOD STANDS One international public health specialist we know refers to these movable feasts as "epidemics on wheels looking for a place to happen." Food at these less-than-sanitary open-air stands is usually left unrefrigerated for long periods of time and exposed to the street soot, gasoline fumes, and heat. Do yourself and your health insurance company a favor and eat only in clean, good-quality restaurants or at your hotel.

Diversions
Exceptional Experiences for the Mind and Body

Quintessential Cancún, Cozumel, and the Yucatán

Among other things, traveling south of the border doubtless has taught you that the real spirit of Mexico lies somewhere between the Maya and *mañana*. If you've tried on the requisite number of sombreros, admired the azure waters of Cancún, and haggled over a colorful serape, you've certainly scratched the surface. You may even have gone parasailing, mixed it up with a marlin, eaten an enchilada, and finally learned how to pronounce Xel-Ha. But, amigos, until you savor the places and pleasures listed below, you haven't experienced the true meaning of "Viva Mexico!"

BALLET FOLKLÓRICO DE MÉXICO In every Mexican town and village, music and dance express the soul of the people. Pre-Hispanic Mexican music, simple and almost hypnotic, was dominated by percussion and wind instruments, and was designed to accompany dances and religious rites; each of the many Indian cultures had its own dances and costumes. In spite of very forceful efforts by the conquistadores to stamp out all traces of indigenous cultures, music and dance survived, mainly because the Spanish clergy realized that these arts could be used as tools for recruiting the heathens into the church. The dances and music didn't really change; what changed was the name of the god to whom they were dedicated. Slowly, Spanish, French, and other European traditions found expression as part of this multicultural heritage. Even today, a church festival isn't considered complete without the performance of brilliantly clad folk dancers.

Although the main *Ballet Folklórico* school is in Mexico City, there are numerous smaller troupes across the nation that faithfully re-create the country's dance in the style and tradition of their ancestors. On Cancún, you can enjoy a whirlwind tour of the entire Mexican republic through one of the *Fiesta Mexicanas* offered at several of the larger hotels. The *Continental Villas Plaza* hotel on Cancún (in the Hotel Zone; phone: 98-831022, or 800-88-CONTI in the US) boasts the best and most complete folklore ballet in town, presented nightly at 7 PM. Tickets include dinner and open bar (domestic wine and beer).

CAVES OF THE SLEEPING SHARKS In the late 1960s, oceanographer Ramón Bravo — Mexico's answer to Jacques Cousteau — discovered an incredible phenomenon just off the shores of his native Isla Mujeres. Deep below the surface of the island's coastal plateau lay an intricate network of wide caverns, which has since gained international fame under the misnomer Caves of the Sleeping Sharks.

Normally beasts of perpetual motion, the man-eating sharks that congregate in these caves become almost totally still and give the appearance of being asleep. In fact, this particular species is incapable of sleeping. A living fossil, the shark is one of the few surviving sea creatures void of the sophisticated breathing system that allows other fish to inhale through their mouth and gills. Instead, the lowly shark must remain in constant motion in order to breathe, thus creating a current of water that carries fresh air through its cavities.

The underwater caves at Isla Mujeres contain constant currents which offer the shark a welcome rest, allowing the ocean to do his breathing exercise for him while he remains stationary. And because of the fossilized fish and coral deposits that surround the caves, the water that passes through them is saturated with concentrated calcium, which produces an almost narcotic effect on the sharks, tranquilizing them into a near stupor. Consequently, divers are able to approach and even *pet* these grim reapers of the ocean floor without fear of attack.

It is an experience that can be had only in the Mexican Caribbean. Warning: Unlike Rip Van Winkle, the sharks don't "sleep" for years on end. They have been known to awaken at very inopportune moments, and become extremely aggressive toward divers. But if your heart is strong, your life insurance paid up, and your nerves intact, you may want to venture below the ocean's surface and meet these real-life *Jaws* firsthand.

CENOTES Geographically speaking, the Yucatán Peninsula is one massive, porous, limestone shelf, suspended over an ocean plateau and pitted by cenotes, sinkholes created by a combination of erosive rains and underground caverns. The limestone is slowly worn away in certain areas until it becomes so thin that it collapses into the water bed below. The result is a deep, usually circular cavity that acts as a natural cistern to collect rainwater.

Because the peninsula has very few lakes and rivers, the cenotes were — and still are — a vital source of fresh water for the natives. The ancient Maya selected the locales of their cities based on the proximity of these sinkholes, and the village cenote came to have a crucial significance for their survival. To appease the sinkhole gods, particularly in times of drought, sacrifices had to be made. Gold necklaces, jade figurines, and even humans (usually young virgins, but sometimes mighty warriors, depending on the personal preferences of the specific cenote deity) were cast into the bottom of the holes to entice the gods to produce rain.

Today, most of the Yucatán's cenotes have been dredged of their early treasures — including the skeletons — and are now popular swimming holes for the native *yucatecos.* the water in the cenotes is frequently crystal clear and extremely refreshing — a perfect place for those who like to plunge themselves into a country's history.

Cenotes come in all shapes and sizes throughout the peninsula. One of the most famous — and inviting — is *Cenote Azul* (Blue Sinkhole), just south of Bacalar. There is also a very beautiful cenote at Xcaret, near Playa del Carmen, which has the added attraction of being connected to a series of underground caverns. An overwhelming favorite is at Dzitnup, on the way to Chichén Itzá (for more information, see *The Yucatán Peninsula: Cancún to Campeche* in DIRECTIONS).

CHICHÉN ITZÁ, Yucatán When someone says that you haven't seen Mexico until you've been to the Yucatán, this is what it's all about. The most famous and complete of the ancient Maya cities, this site is a testament to the engineering genius of the Maya. Here are temples, sacrificial wells, sacred ball courts, reclining idols, and the great El Castillo Pyramid. Stand and face El Castillo, which is topped by a temple to the feathered snake god, Kukulcán (also known as Quetzalcóatl); giant carved heads are at the base of the balustrade. Believe it or not, on the first day of spring and the first day of autumn, the undulating shadows form a serpent's body leading from the temple on top to the carved head on the bottom. It's worth planning your trip around the equinoxes!

DÍA DE LOS MUERTOS (Day of the Dead) Although Mexicans fear and respect death as much as any other peoples, they face it, defy it, mock it, and even toy with it more than most cultures. Never is this more apparent than on November 2, *All Souls' Day* — known in Mexico as the *Day of the Dead* — an eminently Mexican holiday perpetuating a tradition of death and rebirth.

By mid-October, bakeries and markets throughout Mexico are filled with sweets and toys created with death as their theme. Bake shops are piled high with *pan de muerto,* a coffee cake decorated with meringues fashioned into the shape of bones. Children, friends, and relatives are given colorful sugar skulls with their names inscribed on them; death figures shaped from marzipan are on sale at most sweets shops. Verses, called *calaveras,* containing witty allusions or epitaphs, are written about living friends, relatives, and public figures, and by the end of October, shop windows take on a macabre air, with shrouded marionettes and other ghoulish-looking figurines heralding the holiday.

On the actual date, families gather in graveyards to picnic and spend the day with their departed, bringing along their loved ones' favorite foods and drink. Graves are decorated with bright orange *zempasuchil* (marigolds), the flower of the dead; *copal,* an incense that dates back to pre-Hispanic cultures, is burned. The celebration begins with prayers and chants for the dead, and usually ends with drinks to the health of the departed. Homes are decorated in much the same way, with tables filled with marigolds and objects of which the deceased was especially fond.

Commemorating the *Day of the Dead* in the Yucatán takes on extra-special meaning. The spirits of the dearly departed are invited to spend a week's holiday with their living relatives. For each day during their "visit," a plate of food is set out for them alongside a bowl of water. When the week draws to a close, the Yucatecans throw a festive celebration for the deceased with the hope of their return the following year.

GUM FRUIT Although Quintana Roo's main industry today is tourism, the region was once renowned for its chicle, or gum, production. In fact, it was during his travels through the Yucatán Peninsula in the late 19th century that Thomas Adams (Adams Chiclet Gum) first noticed that the native Maya Indians customarily chewed on sticks of dried resin from the sapodilla spruces that flourish in the state's tropical jungles. It occurred to him that this practice might prove popular in the US, and Adams ordered a 2-ton shipment of the resin to be sent to his office back home. Within a decade, Adams had built an entire empire on chicle latex.

The introduction of artificial gum substitutes in the mid-1940s resulted in a collapse of the world chicle market, but even today, Quintana Roo still exports an estimated 500 tons of the sticky resin each year.

The chicle tree also produces a fragrant and fleshy fruit known as the *chicozapote,* which is commonly available throughout Mexico. At first glance, the dark, leathery-skinned gum fruit looks a bit like an overripe eggplant, but under its homely peel lies a sumptuous rosy marrow with an indescribably subtle sweetness. *Chicozapote* does not appear on most menus — particularly those in English — but if you ask your waiter, he can usually produce a sample from the chef's personal larder. If not, you can find *chicozapote* in local fruit markets.

MARIACHI MUSIC Although every region of Mexico has its own special music, none is more associated with the country as a whole than mariachi (the word comes from the French for "marriage").

During Emperor Maximilian's reign, wealthy Guadalajara families, trying to imitate the customs of the court, hired musicians to entertain their guests. Today, mariachis — made up of at least one vocalist, a guitar, bass, violin, and a trumpet or two — are usually hired to serenade girlfriends or to play at special events (weddings, birthdays, anniversaries). Their vast repertoire consists of such sentimental love songs as "Si Estás Dormida," "Las Mañanitas" (the Mexican equivalent of "Happy Birthday," but sung for almost any occasion), "Guadalajara," "La Bamba," or "Cucurrucucu Paloma." The traditional Mexican fiestas frequently held at large resort hotels normally include at least one group of mariachis, and any sizable town will have a few restaurants and bars where they provide the entertainment. On weekends, a mariachi band can be heard carousing along the sidewalks of Avenida Tulum in downtown Cancún City in the late evenings. And despite the heat, they will be dressed to the nines in their close-fitting pants, a pistol hanging from each belt; bolero-type jackets, decorated with silver; and wide-brimmed hats.

XTABENTÚN One of the most popular after-dinner drinks in the region, Xtabentún is touted as being the nectar of the pre-Columbian gods. According to a local legend, this delicious anise-scented liqueur was born of a great Maya romance. Long before the Spaniards ever set foot on the Yucatán

Peninsula, the story goes, a beautiful maiden by the name of Sak-Nicte (White Flower) fell in love with Tolhal, a young warrior of her tribe. Unfortunately, Sak-Nicte's beauty also attracted the interest of the village's cruel chieftain, who demanded the girl for himself. A few nights before Sak-Nicte was to be wed to the evil chief, the young lovers fled their homes and took refuge in the Maya jungle. Lost and hungry, they came across a beehive, from which they took the honeycomb and hid it in a basket made from anise branches. That evening, the gods sent a heavy rain to flood their camp. During the deluge, the rainwater mixed with the honey in the basket, giving it an unusual licorice flavor. The following day, the angry chieftain found the lovers and was about to condemn them to death when Sak-Nicte offered him a drink of the honey-anise mixture. The liquid calmed the chieftain's fury and he promised to let Sak-Nicte marry Tolhal in exchange for the beverage's secret recipe.

Xtabentún is still touted as an aphrodisiac. If you want to savor this delicate bouquet for yourself, it can be ordered in most restaurants and bars straight up or on the rocks with a dash of mineral water. It just might lead to romance.

The Other Yucatán's Best Resort Hotels

Our choices of the best places to stay in Cancún, Cozumel, and Isla Mujeres — resorts where you can bake elegantly under the tropical sun, with no greater exertion than raising your wrist to sip a tall, cool drink — are described in detail in THE ISLANDS chapter. But if you've had your fill of sun and sand (sigh!) and want to see more of the Yucatán Peninsula, there are special havens that offer natural beauty and quality services at a discounted price. Far less populated than the bigger resort towns, these places are frequently enveloped in Maya ruins, uninhabited beaches, and pristine cenotes.

So if you're ready to venture farther into the rich Yucatán landscape, follow our lead. The Maya never had it so good.

CONTINENTAL PLAZA PLAYACAR, Playacar, Quintana Roo Right on the "border" between Playacar and Playa del Carmen, it boasts 2 restaurants, 2 pools, a lighted tennis court, and a spa. There are also a good dive shop and fishing facilities, plus an adjacent shopping arcade and an 18-hole golf course. Each of the 200 units has a private balcony and an ocean view. The beach is wide and tranquil and the service first-rate. Information: *Continental Plaza Playacar,* Playacar Km 62.5, Playa del Carmen, Quintana Roo, Mexico 77710 (phone: 987-30100; 800-88-CONTI in the US).

OASIS MARINA MAR, Puerto Aventuras, Quintana Roo The "in" place for Mexican and US yachtsmen alike, this 275-unit complex is built on the largest marina in Mexico. Originally designed as a time-share property, this is probably one of this area's best bargains: For about the price of a room in any other hotel, guests get an entire apartment with everything from a fully equipped kitchen (complete with microwave), giant closets, and in-room safety box to air conditioning and cable TV. The property also has a swimming pool and 2 first-rate restaurants. Information: *Oasis Marina Mar*, Km 269, Carr. Chetumal, Puerto Aventuras, Mexico 77710 (phone: 987-23376; 800-44-OASIS in the US).

RANCHO ENCANTADO, Bacalar, Quintana Roo A small, intimate resort with a lakeside view that exudes good taste. Every cottage is personally appointed with authentic pre-Columbian artifacts and handwoven tapestries. The gardens — where almost every tree is dripping with orchids in full bloom — are meticulously maintained. And for diners with a conscience, the French fare served in its excellent restaurant is carefully prepared to keep calories and cholesterol down. You can rent a sailboat for the day if you feel like exploring the lagoon. Space is limited, so book well in advance. Information: *Rancho Encantado,* PO Box 233, Chetumal, Quintana Roo, Mexico (phone: 983-80427; 800-221-0555 in the US).

The Yucatán's Natural Wonderlands

For the ecotourist, the Yucatán is a Disney-like parade of tropical plants, fish, birds, reptiles, and mammals. It is a natural laboratory where flamingos come to nest and manatees and dolphins frolic along the coastal waters without the dangers of being netted by fishermen or slashed by propellers of passing motorboats.

Getting a front-row seat to view all of this unadulterated beauty can mean having to trek for several hours through dense jungles or plowing through sand marshes in a four-wheel-drive vehicle, but for the committed nature-lover, the experience is well worth the effort.

The parks and wildlife reserves listed below are open to the public. No hunting or fishing is permitted in these areas, nor are plants or other organic materials allowed to be removed without explicit written authorization from the appropriate agencies. Be sure to pack your insect repellent.

PALANCAR REEF The absolute best for snorkeling or diving. Off the coast of Cozumel, this spectacular series of coral atolls is teeming with spotted moray, snake eels, trumpet fish, bigeye, copper sweepers, grunt, and angelfish. Between the columns of red, yellow, and violet coral are white-sand passageways and intricate caverns.

The entire area has been declared a national park, and it is illegal to touch any of the coral. You can, however, take a bag of bread crumbs to feed the fish; they'll actually come up and eat out of your hand.

Almost any scuba or snorkeling boat in Cozumel will take visitors to Palancar.

CONTOY This federal bird sanctuary is 11 miles (18 km) northeast of the Quintana Roo coast. About 70% of the island's surface is covered with mangrove thickets, 20% is tropical palms, and 10% is rough grass. More than 300 species of migratory and sea birds nest here each year, including the pelican, which has been negatively affected by the use of pesticides and threatened with extinction in other parts of the world.

To get to Contoy, hire a boat on either Cancún or Isla Mujeres. It's at least a 2-hour ride (depending on the craft and the wind factor), much in unsheltered waters, so if you tend to become queasy at sea, don't make this reserve your first choice.

SIAN KA'AN A massive 1.3-million-acre biosphere of jungle, swamp, and coral beach, with a tepid bay tucked away in its center where dolphins and manatees play tranquilly with any human who happens to pass their way. This is the largest nature reserve in the country, and it contains just about every species the peninsula has to offer, from giant boa constrictors and man-eating crocodiles to docile honey bears and risible spider monkeys.

Sian Ka'an lies just south of Tulum on the continuation of Route 307 from Cancún and Playa del Carmen.

RÍO LAGARTOS One of the only three known nesting sites in the world for the salmon-toned flamingo, this marshy reserve is 65 miles (104 km) north of Valladolid in the state of Yucatán.

Amazing Out-of-the-Way Beaches

In addition to the splendid — and sometimes crowded — strands described in THE ISLANDS chapter, happily, there are plenty of virgin beaches in Quintana Roo. Route 307 from Cancún to Tulum is chock-full of undeveloped oceanfront with vacant sun-kissed strands; the best are those that have no signposts. Just follow any dirt path that detours toward the ocean and you may find a secluded strip of sand to call your own for a few hours or even a few days — if you're willing to play Robinson Crusoe for a while. (One favorite hidden cove is Xcalacoco, 30 miles/48 km south of Cancún. There's no sign, but look for a large cement pillar along the roadside and turn off when you get there.)

Those who want the peace and quiet of a private beach with all the modern conveniences will prefer the more beaten paths that lead to Punta Beté, Playa del Carmen, Paamul, Puerto Aventuras, or Playacar. Akumal, headquarters for all Mexican divers, deserves a special mention because it is everything that Cancún could be with about 95% fewer tourists. Chemuyil and Xcacel, both just before Tulum, are little-known bights with tranquil waters and plenty of fringed coconut palms. The beaches along the Gulf of Mexico in the state of Yucatán, such as Progreso, are also great sunning centers, but don't expect to find the turquoise waters of the Caribbean. Instead, the ocean is a deep green.

Scuba and Skin Diving: Dives With a Difference

Mexico's Caribbean boasts some of the finest skin and scuba diving spots in the world. In addition to those mentioned in *Best Depths* in THE ISLANDS chapter, here are our two favorite places to get wet in the wild.

Akumal, a 10-mile-long palm-fringed beach west of Cozumel and south of Cancún, is framed by a large barrier reef. The best diving spots are at *Club Akumal Caribe* and *Akumal Caribe* hotel (both on the Tulum Hwy.), and the *Capitán Lafitte* hotel (at Punta Beté, about 9 miles/15 km north of Playa del Carmen). The waters have 200-foot visibility and stay at about body temperature all year. At 80 to 100 feet, divers can observe magnificent coral gardens, fish, and remnants of 15th-century shipwrecks. The teaching staff at *Club Akumal Caribe* offers excellent instruction, and the club rents all kinds of diving equipment. At Xel-Ha Lagoon, a wildlife refuge just south of Akumal, there is a deep, rock-surrounded inlet where snorkelers can view an endless array of colorful fish (rental equipment available). Skin diving is not permitted.

For subterranean cave diving, the best place to gear up is at the dive center in Puerto Aventuras with Mike Madden, who is credited with having discovered *Nohoch Nachich,* believed to be the largest underwater caverns in the world. The location of these caverns is still not well known; the only way to see them is to arrange a tour through the dive center (phone: 987-22211 or 987-22233). *Note:* This is not an outing for novices. Remember, if you do not hold a C-card from an accredited school, no diving is permitted.

Good Golf

The *Pok-Ta-Pok* and *Puerto Aventuras* golf clubs are described in *Top Tee-Off Spots* in THE ISLANDS chapter. If you want to test your swing along the Yucatán route, set your sights on Mérida; in addition to being a good base for exploring the area, it boasts great greens.

CLUB DE GOLF DE YUCATÁN Francisco Mier y Terán designed this 18-hole course just north of Mérida, formerly known as *La Ceiba*. The sloping hills around the course make judging distances more difficult than on flatter terrains. The greens always look closer than they really are, and even the best golfers have had to readjust their sights after missing a sure shot. Par is 72, but it's hard to make on this course. The manager is José Escalante;

the pro, Angel Lizárraga Pacheco. Km 14 on Carr. Mérida-Progreso (phone: 99-220071).

> **NOTE** Since this is part of a private country club, visitors must obtain special invitations through members, or the state tourist board, to gain access. This may sound complicated, but because the state of Yucatán government is eager to promote its tourism on every front, the formalities of an official invitation are often little more than an obligatory pile of forms filled out in triplicate and left at the Tourism Office in Mérida. For further information contact the Tourist Information Center in the *Peón Contreras Theater* (open daily from 8 AM to 8 PM; phone: 99-249290)

Fantastic Fly Fishing

For aficionados of the sport, some of the best fly fishing can be sampled beyond the resort community.

Fly fishers prefer the area around Sian Ka'an, where the waters are teeming with barracuda, tarpon, red drum, snook, wahoo, and even pompano. Since this area is part of a national wildlife reserve, there's no taking home your trophy to mount on the wall. Chetumal, which used to be a fashionable starting point for fishing expeditions, is still frequented by local anglers, but has very little appeal for the international set. For the best fishing near Progreso head out east toward Chicxulub, where you'll also view several typical fishing villages. If you make it the 18 miles (29 km) to Chicxulub, stop off at the shipyards. This is where the pirate-style ships seen in Cancún are constructed by hand. To the east is Chelem and Chuburna, both renowned for their tranquil abandoned beaches and natural wildlife. This is also a great place to sample grilled duck (in season).

More information on fishing in Mexico, including guides, regulations, fishing seasons, and tournaments, can be obtained by writing to the *Dirección General de Administración de Pesca,* 269 Av. Alvaro Obregón, Mexico City, Mexico 06700 (phone: 5-211-0063).

Camping along Mexico's Caribbean Coast

Perhaps because of its isolation from the rest of the country, the Yucatán Peninsula has been lagging in its development of camping services and facilities. Driving an RV all the way to Cancún or anywhere else on the peninsula is quite an ambitious task in itself. There are a few trailer parks, mostly in Mérida or as a secondary service at a so-so beach hotel, but don't expect them to include playgrounds, washing machines, or any of the other conveniences you may have come to expect.

If, on the other hand, your idea of camping is a sleeping bag under the stars, you will find the Mexican Caribbean far more accommodating. There are many free beaches, and the absence of laws prohibiting camping on public land opens thousands of miles of secluded grounds to hoist a tent. *Beware:* There are *bandidos* who prey on unwary campers.

Also, many of the national parks and wildlife reserves allow campers to spend a night or two, but check first to make sure that no formal permits must be obtained. The administrators of Contoy, for example, allow only overnight stays for organized ornithology groups with prior documentation and authorization from the Secretariat of Agriculture and Hydraulic Resources (SARH), proof of immunization against tetanus, a notarized letter of intent as to the reasons for wanting to camp there, and medical certification by a local physician stating that you are in good general health — a considerable exercise in bureaucracy even by Mexican standards.

Still, there is a special appeal associated with touring an area with your own self-contained accommodations that can be picked up and moved from one day to the next, regardless of whether they consist of an army surplus pup tent or a fully equipped, 3-bedroom Blue Bird.

Hunting

The Yucatán is a hunter's paradise; game is plentiful from the Quintana Roo jungles to the plains of Campeche. With the proper license, hunters can go after wild turkey, most kinds of duck, geese, quail, wild boar, deer, grouse, doves, agoutis, peccaries, and armadillo. A special permit is required to hunt white-tailed deer and gray fox.

Different parts of the peninsula have different types of game. Deer (*venado*), particularly the princely white-tailed deer, are most heavily concentrated in the state of Quintana Roo. Campeche also has deer, but they tend to be *temazate,* a small jungle deer. Quail (*cordonizes*), doves (*palomas*), duck (*patos*) — especially teal, pintail, and mallard — geese (*gansos*), and wild turkey are found almost everywhere in the region. Big-game hunters will have to go as far as Campeche to find fox, but you can still hunt *tepezcuintles* (small wild pigs) in November through December on the island of Tamalcab in southern Quintana Roo. (*Important:* Check an updated list of endangered species before you decide what game to go after. Right now, jaguar, ocelot, puma, and crocodiles are on the endangered list. Your local zoo will be able to help.)

Hunting in Mexico is relatively easy once you've gotten across the border, but there is quite a bit of red tape involved in bringing guns into the country and taking them out again. Moreover, there are a lot more restrictions in Mexico as to the type of weapons allowed. Some arms that are classified as sport rifles in the US are considered lethal weapons in Mexico and can be used and owned only by the military. Not only are arms subject to strict limitations, but so are the number of rounds permitted for each gun. Plan a hunting trip well in advance to allow ample time to obtain the necessary papers. If you enter the country without the proper documentation, your rifles may be confiscated and you may even end up in a Mexican jail.

Hunting seasons and bag limits vary according to the state and the abundance of game each year. For general information in English or Spanish, or for answers to specific questions, permit information, and the official hunting season calendar (*calendario cinegetico*), write to the *Direc ción General de Protección Forestal y Fauna Silvestre, Secretaría de Agricultura y Recursos Hidáulicos* (*SARH*), Progreso 5, Coyoacán, México DF 04110; phone: 5-658-8436. It will supply a current hunting season calendar and an application for hunting licenses or special permits for any game that require them. In order to obtain a special permit, state the game you are after and the season and region in which you will be hunting. (*Note:* Because of the timing, you will probably have to write to the Hunting Bureau *twice:* once to obtain the calendar and list of game requiring special permits, and then again stating which animal you will be hunting, and when and where. It's realistic to start the process at least 3 months before your scheduled arrival in Mexico.)

Every hunter in Mexico must be accompanied by a registered Mexican hunting guide, and each hunter must have a hunting license — a document completely separate from the special permit, which is required only for those going after particular species. But first you must obtain a permit to transport arms temporarily into Mexico. To get this permit, you must present — to the Mexican consulate nearest your American address — a valid passport, a notarized letter from your sheriff or police department stating that you have no criminal record, five passport photos, and a letter asking to take firearms temporarily into Mexico. The letter must state the brand name, caliber, and serial numbers of the arms you intend to take into the country. Hunters are allowed only one high-powered rifle of any caliber, or two shotguns of any gauge. Automatic weapons are prohibited. The Mexican consulate will issue a permit for firearms and a certificate of identity with a description of your weapons. The fee for this service is around $50. To facilitate re-entry into the US, you should, before departure, register firearms and ammunition with US Customs. No more than three nonautomatic firearms and 1,000 cartridges will be registered for one person.

There's more, however. Actual hunting licenses, good only in the state for which they are issued, can be obtained from the *Dirección General de Protección Forestal y Fauna Silvestre, Secretaría de Agricultura y Recursos Hidáulicos* (*SARH*), Progreso 5, Coyoacán, México, DF 04110, or from the local *SARH* office. To obtain a license for hunting birds or small mammals, you must fill out and sign an application, show proof that you have hired a local hunting organizer, pay the fee, and, most important, present your permit to transport arms temporarily into Mexico. "Special permits" are issued only through the Mexico City office of the Wildlife Bureau, and two passport-size photos again are required. Hunting licenses for birds or small animals cost about $20 per state. You also will be asked to register your weapons with the office of the commander of the local military garrison. Costs of licenses for other species vary. A license for hunting bighorn sheep, for example, costs about $5,000! Along with a licensed guide, hunters are required to have a medical certificate of good health in order to obtain the permit to hunt certain species, such as black bear. Once you've made it into the country, obtained your license and permits, tramped through the jungles, and bagged your game, your final task is to get your game out of the country and into the US. First, check bag limits with the Mexico hunting department *and* with US Customs — they're different and they change. Game mammals and migratory game birds require a Mexican export permit or the permission of a Mexican game official. US law requires that a permit be issued from the Fish and Wildlife Service for wild game birds, wild fowl, or wild game animals. Animals may be protected by international law, by US law, or by both. The regulations covering them change periodically, so before going to Mexico, consult the *Division of Law Enforcement* (PO Box 3247, Arlington, VA 22203-3247) and the *Office of Management Authority* (PO Box 3507, Arlington, VA 22203-3507) — both part of *The Fish and Wildlife Service, US Department of the Interior* — about the specific laws and regulations involved in bringing game back into the US.

All of the above deals only with ground transportation. If you enter Mexico by air, and your license and permit are in order, you shouldn't have any trouble with customs.

Some of the red tape can be avoided if you join a hunting expedition to Mexico from the US, or engage a Mexican hunting guide before leaving the US. You can do this through Mexican Consulates or tourist offices in the US (see GETTING READY TO GO), or through local tourist offices throughout the Yucatán.

Below is a survey of the peninsula's best hunting spots listed by state, a general guideline as to what game can be hunted during which seasons, and data as to where to contract guides in each capital city.

QUINTANA ROO Most birds, including ducks, geese, guinea hens, garganeys, quail, and doves, can be hunted during the winter months, from about mid-November through mid-February. The pin-tailed sandgrouse and chachalaca (*ortalis vetula macalli*), on the other hand, nest in the early winter and can be hunted only during the autumn months. Agoutis, rabbit, raccoon, badger, and possum are usually open game in November through January. The *tepezcuintle* season is only about 1 month long, starting sometime in mid-November. You will need a special permit to hunt wild boar (November through December) or deer (October through April), and you will be restricted to killing only adult males of these species.

Because Quintana Roo is now pushing its ecotourism rather than hunting, game limitations are becoming stricter by the day. Make sure you have the latest information on regulations before setting out. Just because you were told 2 months ago that a particular species was fair game does not mean the same rules apply today.

Unfortunately for the visitor to Cancún, Cozumel, or Isla Mujeres, all paperwork must go through the capital city of Chetumal, in the extreme south of the state. On the up side, the south is where the best hunting is found, so it is not that far out of your way to visit the appropriate offices. The SARH offices (at Carr. Escarcega, Km 3.5, Chetumal 77000, Mexico; phone: 983-20500) are open from 10 AM to 2 PM and from 6 to 9 PM, Mondays through Fridays.

STATE OF YUCATÁN Duck-hunting season runs from about mid-December to early March, and the hunting is best on the north and west coasts (especially between Sisal and Celestún). Bobwhite and quail can also be found in the flatlands near Mérida. Trips into the jungle for wild boar and a species of 2-foot-tall jungle deer can be arranged during the month of December.

Local permits can all be arranged in the capital city of Mérida through the local SARH bureau (475 Calle 59, Mérida, Yúcatan 97137, Mexico; phone: 99-239964), open from 9 AM to 3 PM Mondays through Fridays. There are a lot of hunting lodges and clubs in Mérida, which the representative from the SARH bureau will be able to recommend in accordance with the type of game you are after.

CAMPECHE Although the ocelot and the jaguar are protected against hunters under current national law, visitors can still bag big game in Campeche. Gray fox is permissible game during November and December. Most birds can be hunted during the fall and winter months, and small mammals are allowed to be hunted from November through February. Deer season runs from November through April, depending on the species.

The address for the local SARH bureau is Plaza Moch.-Couoh., Centro, Campeche 24010, Mexico (phone: 981-66068).

A Shutterbug's View

If you can get it to hold still long enough, Mexico's Caribbean Coast is an exceptionally photogenic region. The thriving resort cities, the shimmering sea, the beaches, the people, and traces of a rich history that has its roots in pre-Columbian times make the Yucatán a fertile stomping ground for shutterbugs. Even a beginner can achieve remarkable results with a surprisingly basic set of lenses and filters. Equipment is, in fact, only as valuable as the imagination that puts it into use.

LANDSCAPES AND SEASCAPES The Yucatán's spectacular Maya ruins are most often the favorite subjects of visiting photographers. But the region's untamed jungles and Caribbean waters provide numerous photo possibilities as well. In addition to the archaeological wonders at Chichén Itzá, Tulum, and Cobá, be sure to look for natural beauty: Colorful toucans that roost in the marshy *mangares* (swampy mangroves) of overgrown rain forests, mystical cenotes (sinkholes) adorned with alabaster lilies that lead into underwater caverns, the well-manicured plots of flowers at the Plaza de la Independencia in Mérida, the bright orange acacias that line the Paseo Kukulcán in Cancún, the tranquil waters of its Nichupté Lagoon, and the unassuming fishing boats that skim along the waters around Isla Mujeres are just a few examples.

Color and form are the obvious ingredients here, and how you frame your pictures can be as important as getting the proper exposure. Study the shapes, angles, and colors that make up the scene and create a composition that uses them to best advantage.

Lighting is a vital component in landscapes and seascapes. Take advantage of the richer colors of early morning and late afternoon whenever possible. The overhead light of midday is often harsh and without the shadowing that can add to the drama of a scene. This is when a polarizer is used to best effect. Most polarizers come with a mark on the rotating ring. If you can aim at your subject and point that marker at the sun, the sun's rays are likely to be right for the polarizer to work for you. If not, stick to your skylight filter, underexposing slightly if the scene is particularly bright. Most light meters respond to an overall light balance, with the result that bright areas may appear burned out.

Although a standard 50mm to 55mm lens may work well in some landscape situations, most will benefit from a 20mm to 28mm wide-angle. The ruins of Uxmal, with the Sorcerer's Temple and the House of the Turtles looming in the distance, for example, is the type of panorama that fits beautifully into a wide-angle format, allowing not only the overview, but the opportunity to include people or other points of interest in the foreground. A flower, for instance, may be used to set off a view of Mérida's Casa Montejo, or people can provide a sense of perspective in a shot of Cozumel's bustling San Miguel dock and Cobá's magnificent Maxcanxoc stelae.

To isolate specific elements of any scene, use your telephoto lens. Perhaps there's an intriguing carving of the rain god Chac in the Jaguar Temple of Chichén Itzá that would make a lovely shot, or it might be the interplay of light and shadow on the rippling sand at San Francisco Beach in Cozumel. The successful use of a telephoto means developing your eye for detail.

PEOPLE As with taking pictures of people anywhere, there are going to be times in the Yucatán when a camera is an intrusion. For some Maya, a camera is still viewed as a means of stealing a person's soul, and posing for a photograph is tantamount to spiritual suicide. Many of these people will flee at the first sign of a telephoto. On the other hand, the majority of people you are likely to come in contact with are used to the tourist's ever-present third eye. Consider your own reaction under similar circumstances, and you have an idea as to what would make others comfortable enough to be willing subjects. People are often sensitive to having a camera suddenly pointed at them, and a polite request, while getting you a share of refusals, will also provide a chance to shoot some wonderful portraits that capture the spirit of Mexico as surely as the scenery does. For candids, an excellent lens is a zoom telephoto in the 70mm to 210mm range; it allows you to remain unobtrusive while the telephoto lens draws the subject closer. And for portraits, a telephoto can be used effectively as close as 2 or 3 feet.

For authenticity and variety, select a place likely to produce interesting subjects. The beaches of Cancún are an obvious spot for tourists, but if it's local color you're after, visit the nearby town of Felipe Carrillo Puerto, said to have the largest native Maya population in the entire region, or stroll through Cancún's marketplace, where everyone from Aztec-featured fishermen to tawny-skinned Lebanese carpet vendors hawk their various wares. Aim for shots that tell what's different about the Yucatán. In portraiture, there are several factors to keep in mind. Morning or afternoon light will add richness to skin tones, emphasizing tans. To avoid the harsh facial shadows cast by direct sunlight, shoot in the shade or in an area where the light is diffused.

SUNSETS When shooting sunsets, keep in mind that the brightness will distort meter readings. When composing a shot directly into the sun, frame the picture in the viewfinder so that only half of the sun is included. Read the meter, set, and shoot. Whenever there is this kind of unusual lighting, shoot a few frames in half-step increments, both over and under the meter reading. Bracketing, as this is called, can provide a range of images, the best of which may well be other than the one shot at the meter's recommended setting.

Use any lens for sunsets. A wide-angle is good when the sky is filled with color-streaked clouds, when the sun is partially hidden, or when you're close to an object that silhouettes dramatically against the sky.

Telephotos also produce wonderful silhouettes, either with the sun as a backdrop or against the palette of a brilliant sunset sky. Bracket again here. For the best silhouettes, wait 10 to 15 minutes after sunset. Unless using a very fast film, a tripod is recommended.

Orange, magenta, and split-screen filters are often used to accentuate a sunset's picture potential. Orange will help turn even a gray sky into something approaching a photogenic finale to the day and can provide particularly beautiful shots linking the sky with the sun reflected on the ocean. If the sunset is already bold in hue, however, the orange filter will overwhelm the natural colors, as will a red filter — which can nonetheless produce dramatic, though highly unrealistic results.

NIGHT If you think that picture possibilities end at sunset, you're presuming that night photography is the exclusive domain of the professional. If you've got a tripod, all you'll need is a cable release to attach to your camera to assure a steady exposure (which is often timed in minutes rather than fractions of a second).

For situations such as a folkloric ballet performance at the *Continental Villas Plaza* hotel or nighttime cruises on the lagoon, a strobe does the trick, but beware: Flash units are often used improperly. You can't take a view of the skyline with a flash. It may reach out 30 to 50 feet, but that's it. On the other hand, a flash used too close to your subject may result in overexposure, resulting in a "blown out" effect. With most cameras, strobes will work with a maximum shutter speed of 1/125 or 1/250 of a second. If you set the exposure properly and shoot within range, you should come up with pretty sharp results.

CLOSE-UPS Whether of people or of objects such as stone jaguars on the steps of a Maya pyramid, close-ups can add another dimension to your photography. There are a number of shooting options, one of which is to use a 70mm or a 210mm lens at its closest focusable distance. Unless you're working in bright sunlight, a tripod will be worthwhile. If you are very near your subject and there is a good deal of reflective light, it may pay to underexpose a bit in relation to the meter reading.

If you do not have a telephoto lens, you can still shoot close-ups using a set of magnification filters. Filter packs of one-, two-, and three-time magnification are available, converting your lens into a close-up lens. Even better is a special macro lens designed for close-up photography.

UNDERWATER PHOTOGRAPHY The brilliant colors and shapes of tropical marine life and exotic corals that abound in the Caribbean underworld are images you will surely want to preserve in your personal album. In most dive shops around Cozumel and Akumal, for a nominal fee you can rent underwater photographic equipment that will allow you to click the shutter in this watery wonderland. Kodak and Fuji offer disposable underwater cameras that sell for about $20. These cameras, with 24 exposures, can undergo dives of up to 8 feet. Print quality is not the finest, but the price is right.

Most underwater cameras are quite limited as to what they can and cannot do, so don't expect it to have a 120mm zoom attached. On the other hand, you will be surprised at just how close you can get to most underwater subjects without scaring them or chasing them away. Also, although your vision will be somewhat restricted by a cumbersome face mask, images tend to be sharpened by the effect of water, making it fairly easy to catch a clear shot of even a speedy stingray. Unless you bring along supplementary lighting (which also can be rented), you will have to stick close to the surface in order to capture the natural colors of the fish and reefs.

Underwater photography demands a heavy dose of common sense. Remember: an oxygen tank and latex bodysuit do not make you invincible. Don't swim in too close to that electric eel or disturb the slumber of a "sleeping shark" in the underground caves at Isla Mujeres with a sudden flash of your strobe.

In addition to having their own photographic appeal, Cancún, Cozumel, and Isla Mujeres are perfect jumping-off places for shutterbugs who prefer trekking to tanning. The following are some of the Yucatán's most photogenic places.

A SHORT PHOTOGRAPHIC TOUR

CAPTURING THE CARIBBEAN The aquamarine waters of Mexico's Caribbean make for memorable photographic moments. Set against the ivory sands of Cancún's powdery white beaches, the ocean is like a giant crystalline pool, a kaleidoscope of light and color. You probably won't have to go any farther than your hotel balcony to capture an enticing shot of this seductive sea, but if you want to shoot a picture worthy of a magazine cover, your best bet is to put on your hiking shoes and trek over to *El Mirador* lookout point at the Playa Delfines on the way to the airport. Uncluttered by the trappings of modern civilization, this deserted beach is an example of what the rest of Cancún must have looked like 25 years ago; coconut palms and other exotic plants add to the tropical splendor. The best hour to shoot is at sunrise, when dawn is breaking over the Caribbean and the first rays of morning light are reflected in burgundy and amber on the placid cyan waters. Late risers should wait until dusk to capture the fiery red and orange shaded with muted purple. Be sure to use a wide-angle lens. To add a sense of perspective to the picture, include the silhouette of a passing sailboat in the distance. And for a special touch of tropical allure, why not try framing your photo to include an orchid blossom in the corner of your foreground.

CHICHÉN ITZÁ No matter how many times it's been photographed, this mammoth monument of Maya architectural mastery is forever fresh and exciting to professional and amateur shutterbugs alike. El Castillo Pyramid, which dominates the entire site, is the most obvious photo attraction, but the lordly Temple of the Warriors, surrounded by the somber pillars of the Temple of the Thousand Columns, can be an equally inspiring subject. To create a more dramatic image, try pairing two or more subjects in your frame, such as a full shot of the Platform of Venus with the gigantic jaguar head of the Tzompantli Temple dominating the foreground. Or hike over to the partially restored Chac-Mool statue at the ball court and capture the temple's highest tiers towering over the untamed jungles. A wide-angle lens will allow you to keep both the statue and the pyramid in clear focus while affording a sense of the extensive dimensions of the ruins. In order to capture the intricate relief sculptures etched into the columns and stelae, try to plan your photo outing of these ruins for early morning or late afternoon. Also, avoid shooting the temple straight on. Instead, focus on angles that will silhouette the many shapes and forms. Finally, if you don't suffer from acrophobia and your heart and legs can withstand the exercise, try taking your pictures from atop one of the temples. This will give you an overview of the ruins and allow you to backdrop them against an emerald curtain of thick jungle. As a rule, tripods are not allowed at any archaeological sites in Mexico without prior permission from the Anthropological Institute, so opt for fast film.

NICHUPTÉ LAGOON There is nothing more bewitching than the marshy lagoons of the Caribbean's tropical rain forests. Best of all, you don't have to go very far from your hotel to get a glimpse of this exotic natural beauty. In fact, the Nichupté Lagoon is visible from just about any point along the Hotel Zone isthmus. Nichupté offers an ideal alternative for photographers with a passion for afternoon colors. The waters in the lagoon are darker and more mysterious than those of the translucent Caribbean, and the lustrous rays of the setting tropical sun are reflected and re-accentuated in shimmering tones of soft heather and imperial purple.

Try to position your photograph to include a portion of the sky, the lagoon, and at least one other element of interest. Although the unassuming ruins of El Rey across from the *Holiday Inn Crown Plaza* are not particularly impressive in themselves, they make a very stately silhouette when photographed against the marshy lagoon. If you stand slightly to the east of the ruins, you can also capture the intriguing contours of the mangled *mangares* in the distance.

TULUM Tulum has the distinction of being the only Maya city built by the sea, making it a favorite destination for photographers who want to blend nature and archaeology into a single frame. If this is your intention, be prepared to do some fairly serious hiking to the top of the hill where the Temple of the Frescoes and Gran Palacio lead up to the Castle Pyramid; but to capture the sea in your shot, you have to hike down the side of an 80-foot cliff to the white sandy beach to the left. The shrubbery that abounds will add another dimension: a perfect touch of green to the azure and aquamarine tones of the sea.

Directions

Introduction

Until recently, the possibilities of travel along Mexico's Caribbean Coast and through the Yucatán Peninsula were extremely limited. Even for Mexicans, just getting there represented an ambitious trek through marshy, corkscrew jungle roads which often were so consumed with wild underbrush that every few miles the growth had to be slashed with machetes in order to clear a path for a vehicle. Within a matter of days, the tropical jungles would reclaim the territory and hardly a sign would remain that man or woman had even penetrated that region.

Fortunately, this is no longer the case. In the late 1960s, when the Mexican government decided to commercialize the remotest province in the republic (until about 20 years ago, most of the Yucatán Peninsula was still considered a national territory without state status), "Phase One," an all-out development plan backed by public funding, was put into motion. The region's first international airport — and the first runway of any kind in the state of Quintana Roo — was constructed on an obscure tip on the eastern coast, a tiny fishing village and island called Cancún. Roads were cleared and infrastructure facilities, such as electrical generators, phone lines, and water purification plants, were installed. The government also built Cancún's first resort hotels, *Villas Tacul* and *Playa Blanca*. Fast on their heels followed private-sector complexes, with a massive *Club Med* absorbing the island's southernmost tip. Suddenly, Cancún was an international tourist destination and almost-daily charter flights from the US, Canada, Europe, and even Asia were transporting hundreds of visitors to its powdery shores.

But to keep the tourists' interest and to convince them to stay longer, the Mexican government knew that the Yucatán had to offer more than surf, sun, and sand. Convinced that the region's rich archaeological heritage and virgin jungle could give Quintana Roo's fledgling tourist industry the cutting-edge advantage it needed to be able to compete successfully with well-established and better-known destinations such as Jamaica or Hawaii, Mexican officials opted to inaugurate "Phase Two" of its Yucatán promotion program in the mid-1970s. Once again, massive quantities of state capital were funneled into development, this time for clearing roads, restoring Maya vestiges, and building marinas. It didn't take long for private investors to figure out that if Cancún could skyrocket from an unknown fishing village to a major international resort area in less than 10 years, so could other parts of the peninsula. To get US tourists (and their mighty US dollars) to these new "me-too" resorts, highway communication had to be improved, and no small amount of private capital went into leveling, grading, and paving roads.

The big winner, of course, was the tourist, who now could easily journey from one end of the Yucatán to the other, admiring all the mysteries and magic that this remarkable peninsula has to offer — secluded beaches, Maya ruins, flamingo nesting grounds, colonial haciendas, and picturesque villages.

What follows is a general description of the Yucatán Peninsula plus the prime driving routes through the region, including day trips from Cancún to Cozumel, Isla Mujeres, Akumal, and Tulum; and exploration of the Yucatán, from Cancún to Campeche, and from Cancún to Chetumal, near the Mexico-Belize border. Entries describe the highlights of each route, including useful suggestions for sightseeing and dining, plus descriptions of the driving conditions and approximate timetables for coming and going. *Best en Route* lists suggested accommodations at the best available hotels and inns along the way. Detailed maps introduce each itinerary and note the major reference points along the route.

We've made route selections based on our opinions of the most memorable Yucatán sites and sights, and it's certainly possible to string two or all three of these itineraries together for more extensive roaming. For those with less time, following any single itinerary will help you to see the most notable points of interest (and the most attractive accommodations) in any given area.

Driving from Cancún is not difficult. Your best bet is to rent a car in Cancún City (not at the airport, where the price is considerably higher). In fact, arrange to have a rental car delivered to your hotel the morning of your departure. Several international rental firms, as well as some smaller, regional ones, have offices in the city (see *Sources and Resources* in THE ISLANDS). It's best to reserve a car in advance through a travel agent; specify very clearly what kind of vehicle you require. If you are planning to drive as far as the British Commonwealth Republic of Belize, situated just south of Chetumal, you will need a special letter from the rental company granting you permission for the temporary export of the vehicle. Budget travelers can find VW beetles and Nissans within their price range. Those planning a trek through the jungles of Sian Ka'an down to Punta Allen should seriously consider a four-wheel-drive vehicle. For pure indulgence, try a big, air conditioned, automatic Ford, Dodge, or Chevrolet. These are the biggest autos available in Mexico, and they are constantly in demand, which is why advance reservations are so important. Without a reservation, a car that has these creature comforts may not be available, which can make things sticky for drivers who never learned to shift gears. When you get right down to it, air conditioning, too, is more of a necessity than a luxury for most visitors. The Yucatán is hot all the time.

One word of caution about traveling by car anywhere in Mexico: It's always wise for travelers who will be driving on remote country roads (and the Yucatán has more than its fair share of these) to allow sufficient time to reach their destinations well before dark. Few of the roads covered in the driving itineraries that follow are superhighways, meaning it's inevitable that it will take you considerably longer to cover a given segment of ground here than to drive a similar stretch back home. Driving secondary roads in Mexico after dark is not something we recommend; as a matter of fact, it's a risk we earnestly advise travelers to avoid.

Finally, as anywhere in the world, picking up strangers, camping on a lonely beach, or sleeping in a car in some isolated area can invite serious trouble. It takes only a little common sense, and some very basic planning, to make a driving tour of the Yucatán Peninsula both a safe and an especially memorable travel adventure.

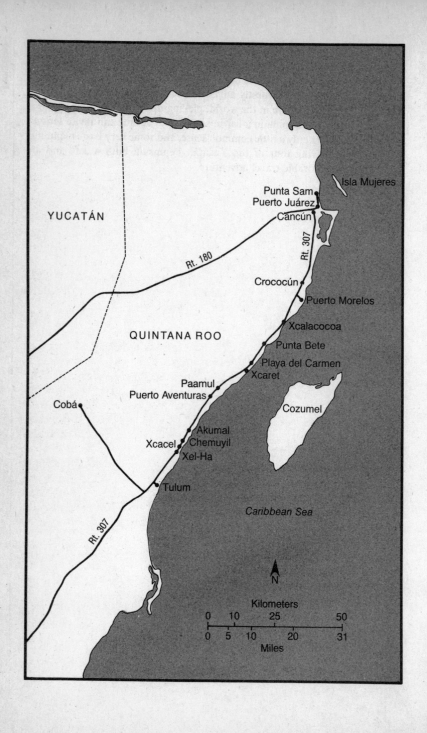

Isla Mujeres

YUCATÁN

Punta Sam
Puerto Juárez
Cancún

Rt. 180

Rt. 307

Crococún

Puerto Morelos

QUINTANA ROO

Xcalacocoa

Punta Bete

Playa del Carmen

Xcaret

Paamul
Puerto Aventuras

Cozumel

Cobá

Akumal
Xcacel   Chemuyil
Xel-Ha

Tulum

Caribbean Sea

Rt. 307

N

Kilometers

0   10   25   50

0   5   10   20   31

Miles

Mexico's Caribbean Coast: Cancún to Tulum

Although Route 307 stretches south from Cancún to Chetumal, many of the points of interest along the way are within easy reach of Cancún and can be seen in a series of individual day trips. The trips outlined below are for those who have had their fill of basking on the beach on Cancún (temporarily, at least), but prefer to pack and unpack only once during a vacation. Though these day trips presuppose a hotel base in Cancún, we offer both hotel and restaurant suggestions for those who opt to continue on to some of the longer routes (see *The Yucatán Peninsula: Cancún to Chetumal* and *Cancún to Campeche* in this section).

DAY TRIP 1: COZUMEL

Despite the fact that many people tend to mentally clump Cancún and Cozumel together as a single tourist destination, they are *not* twin cities. In fact, there is a considerable distance between them — 53 miles (85 km) to be exact (there is a causeway that connects the island of Cancún to Cancún City on the mainland, but Cozumel can only be reached by ferry). Distance is not the only thing that lies between Cancún and Cozumel. There is also an immense wonderland of semi-undeveloped beaches, fishing villages, and sleepy sea coves which are well worth a look. Most commercial tour buses will zip you from Cancún to Playa del Carmen (the town where you catch the ferry to Cozumel) and back again.

However, if you choose to drive, you can enjoy a leisurely tour through small villages — such as Puerto Morelos — and excellent beaches — among them, Punta Beté and Playa del Carmen — and explore this extraordinary stretch of Caribbean Coast. Moreover, there are plenty of unnamed beaches just a few miles off the highway, with no markings other than a well-worn dirt path. With a four-wheel-drive vehicle, you can discover your own "Paradise Found" in the midst of the Yucatán jungles. In the springtime, the area offers yet another bonus for biology buffs: At this time of year, thousands of sea turtles come ashore at night to lay their eggs at Punta Beté, just north of Cozumel — it's a truly impressive sight.

En route from Cancún Going from Cancún to Cozumel is easy. Route 307, a two-lane highway, runs from the south of Cancún (Cancún City) 41 miles (66 km) to Playa del Carmen.

As you head out south from Cancún's Hotel Zone toward the airport on Kukulcán Boulevard, there is a fork in the highway. The road on the right doubles back to downtown Cancún, while the road on the left continues toward the airport. Take the road on the left; within a few hundred feet the highway will divide again. There will be two signs, one pointing right to the airport and the other, on the left, marked "Tulum." Take the Tulum Highway. This will put you on Route 307, and from here on it's straight going to Playa del Carmen.

CROCOCÚN Mexico's only crocodile farm, Crococún is 20 miles (32 km) south of Cancún on Route 307; this should be your first stop on the way to Cozumel. A privately run enterprise operated under the strict watch and auspices of the Secretariat of Agriculture and Hydraulic Resources (SARH), this 60,000-square-foot farm serves as a natural reserve and as a breeding center for the endangered Yucatán crocodile. As recently as 20 years ago, the peninsula was infested with over 10,000 swamp-loving morelete crocodiles, but today poachers and indiscriminate hunters have nearly annihilated the species. Hence, Crococún was founded to replenish the mangrove marshes with specimens of one of the oldest surviving creatures on earth. Eventually, the owners plan to commercialize the crocodile skins, which are internationally prized for their subtle, even-grained belly hides. However, because the reproduction process is so slow (only about 50 eggs are hatched each year), this is definitely a long-term marketing objective. Currently, the ranch has fewer than 500 crocodiles, and SARH will not grant a marketing permit until the population reaches at least 10,000.

One of the more interesting aspects of Crococún is that it is also a biological research center. A few years ago, a local herpetologist discovered that the sex of the moreletes is determined by the degree of humidity and temperature the eggs are exposed to within the nest. Since a slightly lower temperature and dampness will result in the birth of a female crocodile, studies are now under way at Crococún to incubate the eggs under laboratory conditions, thus increasing the female-to-male ratio and speeding up the time it will take to replenish the crocodile stock.

The farm is staffed by veterinary students who, for a small fee, will provide visitors with personalized tours (in Spanish and rather halting English) of the grounds. If you are lucky, your guide will volunteer to mud-wrestle one of the larger reptiles Tarzan-style, and tie its mouth shut so that you can see it up close and caress its tender underbelly. *Don't* try this yourself. Crocodiles can lay totally immobile with their mouths wide open for hours, or even days, but will spring into action as soon as anything that resembles a possible meal approaches.

Also on the farm are white-tailed deer, raccoon (some running wild), spider monkeys, and over 10 species of snakes.

Next door to Crococún is *Acuario Palancar,* a shoddy, aquatic would-be museum which resembles a carnival sideshow trying to cash in on the main event. Inside are 12 aquariums with little more than a miniature turtle, a few goldfish, and a trout or two. Don't waste either time or money on this place.

PUERTO MORELOS About 2 miles (3 km) past Crococún is the turnoff for Puerto Morelos, which is another 2 miles (3 km) east of the highway down a poorly paved path to the coast. Primarily a fishing village, Puerto Morelos is known across the state for its ocean-fresh fish. There is a large coral reef just 500 yards from shore, making it a great place for snorkeling (although not on a par with Cozumel's Palancar National Park). The beaches here usually are empty by Cancún standards, and the dining and accommodations will cost about one-quarter of what they would cost on the resort islands. If seafood is your weakness, here's the place to indulge your taste buds. *Los Pelicanos* (no phone), a casual seaside restaurant on the main drag, has been a favorite dining and watering hole for locals for over a dozen years. *Doña Zenaida* (no phone), a block before you reach the oceanfront, bills itself as "the oldest restaurant in the Mexican Caribbean" and has a good reputation for simple *yucateca* cuisine. For overnight free spirits, visits can include sacking out on the beach near the lighthouse (it's guarded 24 hours a day and is open to the public for camping, but be sure to bring insect repellent and mosquito netting). For those seeking more sybaritic sights, there are deluxe suites at the *Villa Marina* (formerly the *Caribbean Reef Club at Villas Marina*), 2 miles (3 km) south of town (see *Best en Route*).

DR. ALFREDO BARRERA MARÍN BOTANICAL GARDENS Just 2 miles (3 km) south of Puerto Morelos, this state-operated, 50-acre nature preserve is a perfect spot for studying the natural flora of the area. There are several trails for hikers to explore, including one through a gum camp with sapodilla trees, which yield the latex used to make chicle, or gum. There are also thick tropical forests that border a mangrove swamp dripping with wild orchids. Be warned: This is mosquito country, and those who enter without repellent do so at their own risk. On the bright side: Butterflies are in abundance.

Continue south on Route 307 for 8 miles (13 km) to Punta Beté. Halfway there (4 miles/6 km), look for a large cement pillar along the roadside; turn off here to reach Xcalacocoa, a favorite hidden cove.

PUNTA BETÉ Unknown to most Americans, this charming, tranquil beach has been a favorite of well-heeled Europeans for nearly 2 decades. The main attraction, outside the German-run *La Posada del Capitán Lafitte* hotel (see *Best en Route*), is that every May the shores are inundated with thousands of sea turtles laying eggs in the sand. Like salmon and monarch butterflies, sea turtles instinctively return to the site of their own hatching year after year, to lay up to 200 eggs in a single nest under the light of a full moon. If you are lucky enough to witness this extraordinary event, keep your distance: Disturbing the turtles or their eggs is a very serious crime here, usually punishable by fine and imprisonment.

PLAYA DEL CARMEN Just 9 miles (14 km) south of Punta Beté, Playa del Carmen is an underestimated tourist destination. For years, it has been thought of almost exclusively as "the place you take the ferry to get to Cozumel." Recently, however, more discerning travelers have discovered that this port city has merits of its own, including *Las Molcas, the Continental Plaza Playacar*, and the new all-inclusive *Diamond Resort Playacar* hotels. There are also a slew of good restaurants, and some of the most tranquil beaches on the peninsula — all at rates far below their counterparts in better-publicized island destinations.

Playa del Carmen is a good walking town. For those here at lunchtime, the *Chicago Connection* in the north of town satisfies the meat-and-potatoes crowd. *Al Bacco* (2 blocks from the ferry dock) offers fine Italian food in a garden setting, the restaurant at *Las Molcas* hotel (just across from the dock) specializes in seafood, and the *Continental Plaza Playacar* offers two superb restaurants; one of them, *La Pergola,* is now being touted as the best eatery in town.

Adjacent to Playa del Carmen, south of the ferry dock, is the newly developed Playacar community, which promises to become a major tourist destination in its own right. With 2 miles (3 km) of sandy white beach, this 875-acre development is being publicized as a new mini-Cancún; with $1 billion in financing from the private sector, it will eventually include 12 tennis courts, 10 hotels, 3 shopping arcades, and 300,000 private homes and condominiums. To date, only 2 tennis courts and the first 9 holes of an 18-hole golf course are open at Playacar. (The additional 9 holes are due to open this year.) Also in operation are the elegant all-inclusive *Diamond Resort Playacar* and the posh 188-unit *Continental Plaza Playacar* hotel (see *Best en Route*). Nearby is the *Blue Parrot Inn,* the hottest nightspot in town, with live reggae music, inexpensive beer, and rustic accommodations (no phone).

From Playa del Carmen, take a ferry across to Cozumel. (There is no car ferry in Playa del Carmen. Those who wish to take their car to Cozumel must leave from Puerto Morelos; be aware that the wait is long and tedious.) You may leave your car in Playa del Carmen (there is a parking lot directly across from the ferry dock, which is well lighted and quite secure). Passenger ferries to Cozumel leave from the main dock across the street from *Las Molcas* hotel in Playa del Carmen every hour on the half hour from 5:30 AM to 7:30 PM. The ride takes about 45 minutes to an hour, depending on water conditions and the quality and swiftness of the craft. Unless you are particularly fond of long, rocky boat rides, opt for one of the modern, jet-propelled catamarans operated by *Aqua Quin* and *Aviomar.* Their ticket offices are at the dock on the right side. Just opposite them is the ticket booth for the smaller craft. The cost for the jet-propelled ferries will be slightly higher, but the ride is somewhat smoother, and you'll arrive up to 15 minutes faster, which can be a godsend if you don't have your sea legs. (For those prone to seasickness, be sure to bring Dramamine.)

For those determined not to go to sea, air transport via *Aero Cozumel* (phone: 98-842000 in Cancún) is also available, but prices are steep for the quick trip from the mainland. Planes depart Cancún Airport for Cozumel daily at 8 and 10 AM, noon, 2, 4, and 6 PM. For a detailed report on Cozumel, its hotels and restaurants, see THE ISLANDS.

BEST EN ROUTE

The towns and beaches along the route from Cancún to Cozumel are so small that very few have bothered to validate a formal address system. Most of the hotels and restaurants are *conocidos* (known by all). If you are not among the "all" they refer to, ask any local resident to point you in the right direction. For a double room, expect to pay up to $100 at an expensive hotel; $40 to $95 in a moderate one; and $35 or under in an inexpensive one.

PUERTO MORELOS

Villa Marina (formerly the *Caribbean Reef Club at Villas Marina*) A modern, 38-suite facility built especially for water sports enthusiasts. The rooms are big, clean, and air conditioned, with kitchens and an ocean view. There is also a swimming pool, a dive shop, a restaurant, and a bar (phone: 90-987-41147; 98-832636 in Cancún; 800-322-6286 in the US). Expensive.

Plaza Conveniently located on the main plaza, this modest, family-run establishment has 10 rooms with overhead fans, hot showers, and a cafeteria (no phone). Inexpensive.

PUNTA BETÉ

La Posada del Capitán Lafitte A perfect place to get away from it all in style. There are no fans or air conditioning in the 39 bungalows at this German-run resort, but the cool ocean breeze is refreshing enough and the home-cooked dishes are outstanding. In addition to a dining room, there is a pool hall, a swimming pool, a dive shop, a bar — and superb service (phone: 99-230485 or 99-216114; 800-538-6802 in the US). Expensive.

PLAYA DEL CARMEN

Continental Plaza Playacar Located next to the Playa del Carmen ferry dock, this elegant Mediterranean complex has 200 units, 2 restaurants, 2 pools, a tennis court, and a shopping arcade. An 18-hole golf course operated by the hotel's owners is due to be completed early this year (at press time 9 holes were open). All rooms have scenic ocean views, private balconies, satellite TV, and fully equipped kitchenettes (phone: 987-30100; 800-88-CONTI in the US; fax: 987-30105 in Cancún). Expensive.

Las Molcas Located directly across from the ferry dock, this modern 65-room complex is enhanced by a garden of tropical flowers. All rooms are big and air conditioned. There is a good restaurant, 3 bars, a swimming pool, and a boutique (phone: 987-24609). Expensive.

Costa del Mar This 34-room mom-and-pop establishment is at the northern edge of town along the beach. A swimming pool, homey touches, and a terrific restaurant are pluses (phone: 987-20231). Moderate.

Las Palapas Just north of town, these rustic thatch-roofed cottages are a favorite destination for Germans and other Europeans seeking a taste of the tropics with none (or at least very few) of the comforts of home. There is a pool, a restaurant, and a gameroom, but no phone or TV sets. Each cabaña has its own porch with a hammock for lazing away quiet afternoons. A very peaceful setting with a beautiful beach (phone/fax: 5-379-8641 in Mexico City). Moderate.

En route from Cozumel Take the ferry back to Playa del Carmen and pick up Route 307 north to head back to Cancún.

DAY TRIP 2: ISLA MUJERES

Six miles north of Cancún's shore is Isla Mujeres, Quintana Roo's third resort island. At some point, almost everybody staying on Cancún takes a boat over here for lunch and a swim. Passenger ferries to Isla Mujeres leave from the Puerto Juárez ferry dock (approximately 5 miles/8 km north of Cancún City) every hour and a half from 6 AM to 8:30 PM; car ferries leave from Punta Sam (north of Puerto Juárez) from 7:15 AM to 10 PM. Although the *Tranportes Turísticos Magana* craft are a bit run-down, they are dependable (if not always prompt) and cost about $2 per person and $6 per vehicle. The crossing takes 20 to 30 minutes and can be rough for even seasoned sailors.

Those who prefer to make their own itinerary can usually find small private craft at Playa Linda or Playa Langosta that ferry guests across to Isla Mujeres for about $15. Also, you can sometimes arrange with a local fisherman to take you between either Cancún or Cozumel and Isla Mujeres for about $4 one way.

Many people stay overnight on this very small island. The downtown section is a mere 5 blocks wide and 8 blocks long. Most of the streets are unpaved, and there are very few cars. Extremely informal and completely relaxed, it's popular with younger folk; the island attracts an arty, intellectual crowd who stays on until money runs out.

Isla Mujeres is known mostly for its great swimming and snorkeling. Day-trippers should be sure to get to El Garrafón (the Jug), a spectacular national park and beach sheltered by a long coral reef. Here, the fish are larger, and you can swim through schools containing thousands of them. Treat yourself to a fresh seafood lunch at *Ciro's Lobster House* (11 Matamoros, in town; phone: 987-20102), or *Hacienda Gomar* (on the west side of the island on the road to El Garrafón; no phone). For a detailed report on the island, its hotels, and its restaurants, see THE ISLANDS.

En route from Isla Mujeres Take the ferry to return to Cancún.

DAY TRIP 3: AKUMAL, TULUM

This route takes in Akumal, one of the best snorkeling and scuba diving spots along Mexico's Caribbean coast, and Tulum, with its rich archaeological treasures. The beach at Xcaret and the luxurious Puerto Aventuras resort are also on the route, as are the turtle-breeding grounds at Paamul.

Akumal is a seemingly endless breadth of seductive white-sand beaches, spattered with a medley of sheltered coves, Maya ruins, and resort hotels. Snorkelers will be lured to the crystal-clear waters of Xcaret and Xel-Ha's natural aquarium. Full-fledged scuba pros will prefer the promise of sunken treasures off the Akumal coast (rental equipment is readily available). The scholarly anthropologist may even be able to ignore the serene call of the Caribbean shore and make a beeline for the magnificent walled ruins of Tulum and the jungle-enshrouded mysteries of Cobá. Whatever your particular fancy, you will no doubt find it realized along this incredible strip of beachfront paradise.

En route from Cancún Route 307 follows the coastline for 81 miles (130 km) straight into Tulum. From there, your only dilemma will be deciding which way to continue. To the northwest, 26 miles (42 km) away, lies Cobá, a massive collection of unexplored Maya structures swallowed up in untamed jungles; this is the largest archaeological site in Mexico. The process of reclaiming this ancient city (thought to date from AD 600 to 900) has only just begun. Archaeologists believe some 6,500 structures once stood here. Already uncovered are a 130-foot pyramid, a 9-tiered castle, and remnants of a ball court.

The city is believed to have been a trade center, connected by a network of highways with other major Maya cities such as Chichén Itzá and Uxmal. Although there is evidence that Cobá was in use up to the time of the Spanish Conquest, the Spaniards never discovered the site, with the result that it was abandoned and forgotten.

The main highway (Route 307) continues down into the controversial no-man's-land, where pirates and rebels have disregarded the voice of authority since early colonial days. If time permits, try to squeeze a glimpse of each of these attractions into your holiday schedule.

XCARET This once secluded little beach is now one of the most popular sunbathing sites in the Mexican Caribbean. Xcaret (pronounced Shkah-*ret*), 4 miles (6 km) past Playa del Carmen on Route 307, is a happy blend of ancient ruins and sun-kissed (often crowded) beach with an extra helping of cenotes (sinkholes) and underwater caves. A new dolphin pen offers visitors the opportunity to swim with nature's most intelligent aquatic mammals.

There isn't much academic data available on the ruins at Xcaret, because for as long as anyone can remember, they have been in the hands of the Gómezes, a local family that exploits the popularity of the place by charging a token fee to visitors. Although hardly majestic, the ruins are interesting. At the entrance to the grounds is a short base of what must have been a pyramid encrusted with geometric figures and abstract animal motifs. A short distance beyond this structure are two extremely deep cenotes, apparently once used for dumping virgins down to the lustful gods of the underworld in exchange for bumper harvests. Because the structures are so close together, the obligatory archaeological rounds can be completed in less than half an hour; then proceed down the dirt trail to the enchanting little limestone cove at the water's edge. Here, even those who are too lazy to don a snorkeling mask can see the schools of golden damselfish that call these waters home.

But a visit to Xcaret doesn't end with the cove. Up the hill past the cove there is the open-air *Xcaret Café,* which serves a tangy sea snail ceviche and fresh-baked banana bread; beyond is a 50-foot cenote enclosed in the mouth of a cavern. Plunge into the cool, sweet water of this natural pool to wash off the salt from the ocean. Intrepid divers can also explore the various grottoes and crevices of the caves, which extend underwater for about 1,500 feet (rental equipment is available at the dock in nearby Akumal).

There are no hotels at Xcaret, but if you bring your own sleeping bag, you can camp out near the ruins in exchange for a small contribution to the Gómezes' personal nest egg. There are restrooms and shower facilities on the grounds, which Mrs. Gómez keeps extremely clean.

PAAMUL Nowhere else on the peninsula do so many giant sea turtles come to nest. Every spring thousands of these gawky, slow-moving reptiles waddle ashore to lay their eggs in the soft, powdery sands of Paamul (6 miles/10 km past Xcaret), and within a few weeks, the tiny offspring hatch and scurry into the turquoise ocean waters to begin the process anew. The amazing part of this annual breeding ceremony is that somehow the turtles instinctively return each year to the place of their birth to renew the age-old cycle. Those who want to witness this dramatic event can catch a ringside seat in Paamul between May and July, depending on the species.

There are three main types of sea turtles in Quintana Roo — the hawksbill, the *caguama,* and the *blanca* — and they all nest at Paamul.

The turtles usually come ashore in the late evening and burrow themselves into the sands headfirst. Once totally submerged, they release their eggs, up to 150 at a time. The entire process takes about an hour; at the end the turtles quickly return to the sea without a moment's concern for the fate of their progeny. Sadly, most of the eggs will not hatch. Instead, they will be eaten by predator crabs, birds, or insects.

Until recently, turtle eggs were also the unfortunate prey of man — who considered them a delicacy — but under current Mexican regulations all sea turtles and eggs are now protected — at least from humans. Despite these laws, there are still folks who traffic in turtle products ranging from tortoiseshell jewelry to turtle egg soup. The tab for their nefarious merchandising may well be the extinction of the slow-footed beast. Say no to anyone who tries to sell you turtle products.

The overnight accommodations in Paamul are not nearly as swank as in Punta Botó, but there is an 8-unit provincial inn with hot showers, overhead fans, and a restaurant (see *Best en Route*).

PUERTO AVENTURAS Once you've had your fill of roughing it with the sea turtles, bask in pampered luxury at Puerto Aventuras, just 3 miles (5 km) past Paamul and 13 miles (21 km) past Playa del Carmen on Route 307. This swank, high-priced resort is one of the most exclusive in the Mexican Caribbean. Deluxe facilities include the largest marina in Mexico with 250 slips, an 18-hole golf course built around several pre-Columbian structures and a couple of ancient cenotes, a tennis club, and two fashionable waterfront hotels. The larger property, the *Oasis Marina Mar,* a 309-unit, Mediterranean-style complex, is set on its own beach and includes private villa-like suites replete with everything from microwave ovens to double oversized bathtubs (see *Best en Route*). The living is easy, but don't expect these select accommodations to be gentle on the pocketbook. Puerto Aventuras was built as a posh oasis for Mexico's well-heeled elite with discerning palates.

The marina, a yachtsman's dream come true, is located on a turquoise cove that is fed by underground springs, keeping the water crystalline fresh, despite the large number of craft docked here. It has a mooring capacity of 250 slips, for yachts up to 160 feet long. Landlubbers will be attracted to Puerto Aventuras's scenic landscaping, which incorporates the natural beauty of the region with transplanted Asian palms, and orchids brought from the Brazilian Amazon. There is also a private museum, the *Pablo Bush Romero CEDAM,* displaying 18th-century silver goblets, gold coins, medallions, cannons, and other relics salvaged from the *Matanceros,* a Spanish merchant ship that sank off the coast of Akumal in 1741. There are also several Maya figurines that were found at the bottom of surrounding cenotes (sinkholes) used for sacrificial purposes. Open Wednesdays

111

through Mondays from 9 AM to 5 PM. No admission charge. Eastern end of Malecón de la Marina.

Puerto Aventuras is also one of the few places in the world where the public can actually swim with a dolphin. Here's a once-in-a-lifetime thrill to splash and play in the ocean with these beautiful creatures (phone: 987-22211 or 987-22233).

Divers with an urge for something out of the ordinary may be interested in trying their hand at cave diving. *Mike Madden's* dive shop (phone: 987-22211 or 987-22233) at the *Club de Playa* hotel will provide guided tours of the nearby *Nohoch Nachich Caverns* to qualified divers. Discovered in 1987 by Madden, these caves have 43,600 feet of surveyed underwater passages, and are the longest underwater cave system in the world. For more information, see *Scuba and Skin Diving* in DIVERSIONS.

For a casual lunch in a safari-like atmosphere, try the *Papaya Republic,* run by the vagabond son of one of Mexico City's better-known upper class families. For more formal fare, try *Carlos 'n' Charlie's* (a member of the ubiquitous chain), serving everything from spicy barbecued spareribs to chicken Kiev.

AKUMAL Akumal is just a few minutes south of Puerto Aventuras, 5 miles (8 km) away on Route 307. Originally part of a private copra plantation, Akumal gained international status in 1958, when a diving exploration headed by Pablo Bush, a Mexican philanthropist, stumbled across the sunken remains of the *Matanceros,* a Spanish galleon that was lost at sea more than 2 centuries ago. Since then, the place has become an unofficial scuba and snorkeling headquarters for the not-so-idle rich called the *Mexican Underwater Explorers' Club.* When the club was first founded, its members flew down in private aircraft to put on wet suits and scuba tanks for expeditions to the sunken wreck of the *Matanceros;* later they came upon submerged Maya ruins in places where the sea had swallowed up the land.

Today, Akumal is open to the public, and *Club Akumal Caribe* (see *Best en Route*) is a lovely hotel with grounds that contain cannons recovered from the ancient wreckage. There are also several smaller, European Plan hotels in town, mostly geared to hearty meals and no-frills sleeping quarters to accommodate the diving crowd.

For those who want just a taste of adventure, Akumal has an underwater museum where coral-encrusted anchors and guns lie among the rocks much the way they originally were found.

Those who prefer the real thing will want to don their scuba equipment and head into the placid ocean. The Akumal reef, with its towering coral buttresses, is alive with over 300 types of tropical fish, and every now and again a lucky diver will encounter a tarnished button or sand-encrusted coin. Inexperienced divers can learn from the best here, since every other person you meet is a scuba pro. However, a diver's certificate card is required to rent tanks or charter a boat.

There are dive shops on virtually every corner and a few convenience stores that stock beer, wine, and snacks. That's just about it. There is no swinging nightlife in Akumal, only a pearly white beach and azure waters where visitors can luxuriate in the tropical sun under a leafy coconut palm.

CHEMUYIL This relatively unknown beach (sometimes crowded on weekends), 6 miles (10 km) past Akumal on Route 307, is about as close to a Paul Gauguin landscape as you can get in Mexico. Sisal hammocks strung casually between palm trees and exotic drinks served in fresh coconuts make this out-of-the-way little club a whimsical spot where anyone can lounge for a few hours of Robinson Crusoe grandeur. There are also camping facilities, and a charming hotel with 10 suites and 12 tents for campers. For further information, write Don Lalo Román Chemoir Fidecomiso, Xel-Ha, Tulum, Q.R., Mexico.

XCACEL Another perfect little slice of virgin waterfront 2 miles (3 km) south of Chemuyil along Route 307, Xcacel (pronounced Shka-*sell*) is waiting for someone to build a resort on it and make a fortune. For the moment, visitors lucky enough to discover this secluded stretch of sand can still enjoy its peace and serenity.

Just 2 miles (3 km) south of Xcacel on Route 307 is Xel-Ha.

XEL-HA This lagoon — really a series of lagoons — forms a natural aquarium filled with colorful tropical fish and turtles. Xel-Ha (pronounced Shell-*Ha*) used to be a great place for novice snorkelers to test their fins, but daily caravans of commercial tour buses have tended to erode its innate beauty. Too many tourists and too little upkeep have led to the once-transparent waters becoming clouded with murk and debris. This is clearly a case of paradise lost.

While the natural aquarium may not have much allure anymore, there are several scattered ruins on the grounds of this national park that are interesting, if uninspiring. The main structure, a 10-minute hike over jagged limestone terrain, is the Temple of the Birds, where a faint image of Chac, the rain god, and several plumed flamingos can be discerned in the western wall.

Continue south on Route 307 for 12 miles (19 km) to Tulum.

TULUM The crowning glory of any coastal drive (81 miles/129 km south on Route 307) from Cancún is Tulum. Although small, the archaeological zone south of Xel-Ha, with some superb Maya buildings, a beautiful setting, and slightly mysterious air, is a compelling destination.

In fact, this was one of the few cities that was still inhabited when the Spanish arrived. Juan de Grijalva described sighting it from his ship in 1518: "A city so large that Seville would not have seemed more considerable." Little of that metropolis remains, but what there is fascinates scholars. Tulum is the only Maya city known to have been encircled by a walled fortification. It is also one of the few Maya sites on the seacoast.

Apparently, the site was founded hundreds of years before the Christian era began, yet it survived long after other Maya cities had been abandoned. To some, this would indicate that the wall and seafront location were a good idea. The formation that the Spaniards called El Castillo (The Castle) is the zone's most curious structure — a pyramid topped by a small temple with simple columns marking the entrance. Walk carefully to the side facing the sea for a stunning view of white, sandy beaches at the bottom of 80-foot limestone cliffs. About 400 yards offshore is a "blue hole," the ocean equivalent of a cenote. The Temple of the Frescoes contains rare Maya paintings, but Tulum's most famous building is the Temple of the Descending God; over its main door is a large cleaved sculpture of a winged deity plummeting headfirst toward the sea. The conventional theory is that it represents the rain god; an alternative theory is that it represents a descending spaceman.

There are a total of 60 structures at the site, and they can all be seen in about 2 hours of walking. In addition to its Maya paintings, the Temple of the Frescoes bears traces of the original paint on carved limestone statues, still detectable by the discerning eye. There are also several platforms once used for dances, funerals, and ancient ceremonies.

Tulum offers some natural amenities as well. The beach just below the site is beautiful. The local waters can be fished year-round, and hunting in the jungle is quite good. Four major duck migrations rendezvous here each year. Wilder game include boar and deer.

En route from Tulum Head north on Route 307 to return to Cancún.

BEST EN ROUTE

Prices along the Caribbean Coast are often high — especially considering the often rustic (or worse) accommodations available along the way — even outrageous by US standards. Those areas (such as the scuba divers' haven at Akumal) enjoying "favorite resort" status often charge more for less, while other, as yet undiscovered regions offer elegant accommodations at down-to-earth prices. A double room in Puerto Aventuras or Akumal, for example, will run at least $120 a night and, depending on the season, may start at $150 a night. You can rent a cabin in Paamul, on the other hand, for about $60 a night. Tulum is a vacationer's bargain, with rustic cabañas going for about $40 a night. Don't be surprised, though, if the electricity runs only part-time.

PAAMUL

Cabañas Paamul An 8-cottage complex with hot showers, overhead fans, and a small restaurant; all of the cabins open onto the beach for a ringside view of the spring turtle parade. Km 85 on Rte. 307 (phone in Mérida: 99-259422). Moderate.

PUERTO AVENTURAS

Oasis Club de Playa The first hotel to be completed at this recently built resort, the 36-room building is exquisite, but the accommodations are not as luxurious as at the *Oasis Marina Mar*. There is a swimming pool, air conditioning, and a restaurant (phone: 987-23376 or 987-23287; 800-44-OASIS in the US; fax: 987-23332). Expensive.

Oasis Marina Mar A 309-unit, super-luxury complex with fully equipped kitchens, air conditioning, a swimming pool, cable TV, and 2 restaurants (phone: 987-23376 or 987-23287; 800-44-OASIS in the US; fax: 987-23332). Expensive.

AKUMAL

Akumal Cancún Right on the beach, it has 81 air conditioned rooms with terraces, 11 two-bedroom suites with kitchenettes, a pool, 2 lighted tennis courts, all water sports, a dive shop, a disco, 2 restaurants, a video bar, and miniature golf (phone: 98-842272 or 98-842641 on Cancún). Expensive.

Club Akumal Caribe Formerly a private club for well-heeled divers, this lovely 61-room place is now open to the public. Near Tulum and Xel-Ha, it's also a fine spot for lunch (phone: 98-841975 on Cancún; 987-22532 on Cozumel; 800-351-1622 in the US). Expensive.

TULUM

Ana y José The most comfortable accommodations in the vicinity, this 15-unit inn has provincial charm and overhead fans. The gardens which surround the red tile buildings are particularly inviting. Km 7 on Rte. 307 to Tulum (phone: 987-41117). Inexpensive.

Sian Ka'an Ocho Oasis At the entrance of Sian Ka'an Wildlife Reserve, this complex of thatch cabañas is an exceptionally clean little spot with a great ocean view and a restaurant that specializes in vegetarian dishes. On the down side, there is no air conditioning and the electricity is on for only a few hours a day. No phone. Inexpensive.

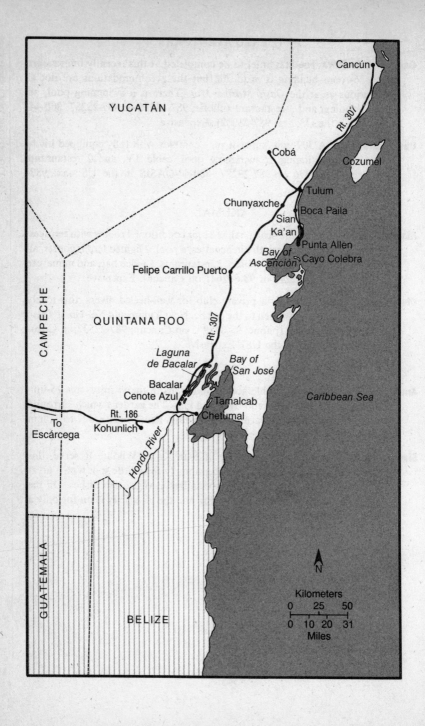

The Yucatán Peninsula: Cancún to Chetumal

The southern coast of Quintana Roo — which stretches from Cancún to Chetumal — is a peculiar blend of blissfully tranquil beaches and untamed jungle that served as the backdrop for one of Mexico's bitterest conflicts, the Castes War. The highway that leads to Chetumal, the capital of the state of Quintana Roo, was once a road paved with the blood of Maya Indians and Spanish colonists.

Isolated and largely ignored by the rest of the country, and even the rest of the peninsula, southern Quintana Roo (pronounced Kin tah-nah Row) is nonetheless strategically important from a military standpoint because of its location on the Bay of San José and its proximity to Guatemala and Belize (both of which have at one time or another tried to lay claim to the region). The Maya also recognized the significance of this remote area and were slow in relinquishing it to the Spanish aggressors. Unlike their brothers in the north, the southern Chetumal Maya refused to submit to the Spanish throne. In fact, this was the last section of Mexico to fall from Maya hands.

Economically, the region had much in its favor: rich copra orchards, abundant logwood (used for making dye), mahogany forests, and fertile sugarcane fields. There was also enough land for anyone who was willing to work it, and a general sentiment of indifference toward the law. This factor attracted social and political deviants as well as wide-eyed fortune hunters and rough-and-tumble buccaneers.

During the 18th and 19th centuries, with little or no intervention from the local sheriffs and plenty of open seashore to transport undeclared and unlevied goods, many a southern Quintana Rooer found himself engaged in the import and export of unsavory cargoes, including weapons, drugs, and even slaves. This brought prosperity, and with it an onslaught of unsolicited visits by pirates, looters, and carpetbaggers. The bloodletting in this region was so prevalent that at one time the entire population of southern Quintana Roo was reduced by 80% in a single year.

When Quintana Roo gained statehood in 1974, the Mexican government decided to instill a semblance of law and order in the region by clamping down on the transport of contraband, drugs, and other illegal trade. The notorious brothels and opium dens in Chetumal's red-light districts were closed down and an all-out effort to register the local citizenry was launched. Despite an ambitious effort, the undertaking was only partially successful. The brothels moved to new addresses, and those people who did not want to be on the official registries simply took refuge in the jungles during the census taking.

Today Chetumal, Quintana Roo's capital, is a hodgepodge of flashy lights and shady activities, a poor man's New York in the tropical jungle. Despite a veneer of respectability, the city has always managed to keep itself just outside the reach of the long arm of Mexican law.

Driving through this area is a stimulating experience. The beaches are less traveled — and less spoiled — than those in northern Quintana Roo. Giant sea turtles, now almost extinct throughout the world, can be seen almost everywhere along the coast laying their eggs in the moonlit sands during early spring. This is a land that still belongs to nature. Man has only brushed the surface of the vast Quintana Roo jungles, where ocelots, crocodiles, and howler monkeys still roam wild in their native habitat. Even the homely, cumbersome (yet somehow endearing) manatee, rarely seen anywhere else on earth, playfully romps in the brackish waters of the Bay of Ascención and Hondo River. Fishermen find this region an angler's paradise, where bonefish, snook, and the succulent pompano almost leap onto their hooks. The two largest Maya archaeological sites in the state, Tulum and Cobá, are also along this route, as is the Sian Ka'an Wildlife Reserve, which occupies a full 1.2 million acres of jungle, marsh, and coral beach.

The roads are surprisingly good, particularly compared with the highway that leads to the Yucatán state border. The 239-mile (382-km) drive from Cancún to Chetumal can take only about 4 to 5 hours, but with so much to see in between, wiser travelers allow several days.

En route from Cancún Route 307 follows the coastline for 81 miles (129 km) straight into Tulum. For a detailed report on the route to Tulum, points of interest, and hotels and restaurants along the way, see *Mexico's Caribbean Coast: Cancún to Tulum,* in this section.

The route from Tulum to Chetumal can be covered in about 3 hours. But if time allows, two side trips — each requiring a return to Tulum before continuing on to Chetumal — are well worth considering: a day trip from Tulum 26 miles (42 km) northwest to Cobá, and a day trip (or a possible overnight stay) 36 miles (58 km) south to Punta Allen. There are other options on the way to Chetumal: You may choose to stop off for the night in Bacalar to savor the beauty of its peaceful, multihued lagoon. The Kohunlich archaeological zone 36 miles (58 km) west of Chetumal is also worth viewing, and should take about 2 hours to tour comfortably.

Just past the Tulum exit on Route 307, there is a turnoff on the right for the unnumbered road northwest to Cobá. This 26-mile (42-km) highway is paved and, although not as smooth as Route 307, quite drivable.

COBÁ Cobá is Quintana Roo's largest archaeological site; to get a reasonably complete survey of it, count on a full-day visit. There is only one hotel near this 81-square-mile Maya site: the rather austere *Villa Arqueológica,* run by Club Med (see *Best en Route*). But those who decide to spend the night probably will be more interested in playing Indiana Jones and cutting through the unexplored portions of Cobá than worrying about delivery of breakfast from room service.

The formal name of this classic Maya city is Cobá Kinchil, which translates as "Waters Stirred by the Winds at the City of the Sun God" — a rather cumbersome moniker by any standards. The massive city was first noted by Teobert Maler in 1897, and explorations began between 1926 and 1930. The site was opened to the public in 1973 when the road leading to it was paved; major excavations were started in 1974.

Unlike the rest of the peninsula, the Cobá area is endowed with five natural lakes, which apparently allowed the ancient Maya to irrigate their fields and live in relative comfort. Not surprisingly, the city maintained a large population, perhaps as many as 50,000 people. Experts estimate that there are at least 6,500 structures buried in the all-consuming jungles of Cobá, but only a few of them have been charted and restored. Even more impressive than the number of buildings is the complex network of *sacbes,* or roads, that linked the main groupings (6 in all) to one another and extended out to other Maya cities. There was even a 12-foot-wide *sacbe* that led as far as Chichén Itzá, some 56 miles (90 km) to the northwest through the densest rain forests on the peninsula.

The 120-step Nohoch-Mul Pyramid, the tallest pre-Columbian structure in the Yucatán, is the highlight of a trek through Cobá, but the august Maxcanxoc stelae are strong contenders for any visitor's attention. The eight 8-foot-high monolith tablets are intricately carved with finely crafted relief figures.

Because it is such a sprawling site, getting from one end of Cobá to the other is a complicated and lengthy process, and possible only on foot — so make sure to wear sensible shoes or, better yet, hiking boots. Insect repellent is also advised. The jungles still govern the park, and mosquitoes, gnats, and ticks are everywhere. Travelers wishing to continue on this route must return to Tulum before setting out for Chetumal. Those opting to take a second side trip to Punta Allen must also return to Tulum.

For a side trip to Punta Allen, take Route 307 south from Tulum. There are signs indicating a turnoff onto an unnumbered road south to Punta Allen. The 36-mile (57-km) drive will become, after a few short miles of pavement, an uneven (sometimes rutted) jungle road. It's well worth it, however, because along the way is Sian Ka'an (pronounced Shahn-*can*), Mexico's prized national wildlife preserve — an ecological wonderland teeming with reptiles, mammals, and a rain forest.

SIAN KA'AN In January 1986, a 1.3-million-acre biosphere of virgin jungle, swamp, salt marsh, coral beach, and mangrove forest in east Quintana Roo was declared a national wildlife reserve by presidential decree. Mexico's largest federally protected area, Sian Ka'an (which translates as "Place Where the Sky Is Born") is an ecotourist's paradise, where over 320 species of birds and 68 different types of reptiles and mammals flourish and multiply in their natural habitat. For those who want a taste of the jungle and are willing to endure the harsher side of nature, Sian Ka'an is a delectable adventure into an untamed wonderland. An overland excursion along the jungle path can mean coming face-to-face with a giant boa constrictor, a curious spider monkey, or a glimpse of a sprightly ocelot startled into action by the sound of a car motor. Those who go deep enough into this bewitching rain forest may even have a chance to romp in the Bay of Ascención with a couple of inquisitive manatees or a congenial dolphin. A 2-hour canoe trip through a series of lagoons shrouded by webbed vines can even mean an opportunity to survey unexplored pre-Hispanic ruins dating from up to 20,000 years ago.

Driver beware: The road into Sian Ka'an is unpaved and generously pitted with potholes. The 36-mile (58 km) drive to Punta Allen, where the road terminates at the Bay of Ascención, takes at least 3 hours to navigate in good weather. Moreover, the jungle literally closes in as you proceed, and there are times when your vehicle will actually have to slice its way through the overhang and palm trees. Sudden thunderstorms are common (they don't call them tropical rain forests for nothing), and there are giant puddles in the road large enough to swallow a VW beetle. Stop your vehicle frequently and test the terrain ahead on foot to be sure you won't end up in a mass of quicksand or swamp quagmire. Insects are also a problem, and repellent and long sleeves are highly advised. The heat is sometimes stifling in the murky jungles, and the stench of organic decay around the stagnant marshlands often is overwhelming.

That said, for those still determined to undertake an expedition into Sian Ka'an, there are a few basic guidelines to follow. First, gas up at the filling station near the Cobá exit. At the same time, make sure your car's fluid levels are good and let about 5 pounds (more for heavy-traction vehicles) out of the tires so that they will ride more easily over the jungle terrain. Picking up a couple of bottles of drinking water is also a good idea. Almost any vehicle in good condition can endure this journey, but four-wheel-drive jeeps are much more suited to the topography. The adventurous type (a foregone conclusion for the traveler willing to embark on this venture) may even want to purchase some food and soft drinks to stage a jungle cookout and picnic along the ocean shore.

For those with an urge to play Tarzan along the way, there are several rustic cabaña-style cottages with hammocks, running water, and electricity during certain hours of the day (don't try to plug in an electric razor; the light here is battery-powered, 12 volts, direct current). The best of these primitive little makeshift guesthouses is the *Posada Cuzan* in Punta Allen, run by Sonia Lopez, a New York anthropologist turned Sheena (see *Best en Route*). She whips up a delicious potluck dinner (usually lobster tails sautéed to perfection in local herbs) for a pittance, and can offer firsthand information about what to see and how to get there.

Unlike many nature reserves, Sian Ka'an combines the protection of wildlife with the balanced use of resources and the cooperation of local inhabitants. This "holistic" approach to the preservation of the nation's natural heritage, without the forced relocation of indigenous populations that have lived on and worked the land for centuries, reflects a relatively new stance in finding a practical equilibrium between ecological concerns and economic realities. The reserve is divided into three sections, each with its own restrictions regarding exploitation by humans. Along the edges of the reserve there is a 10-mile-deep buffer zone where those families who have ancestral ties to the region (about 1,000 people in all) are allowed to continue their traditional vocations as fishermen and hunters. There is also a gathering zone where these people are allowed to collect the plants they use for dietary or medicinal purposes. Only government and private-sector researchers and ecologists are allowed to enter the highly protected core zone of the reserve.

The end result of this experimental policy is that the indigenous inhabitants of the region are working hand in hand with the scientists to find better ways of protecting the local flora and fauna. Rather than trying to stop the commercialization of crocodile hides, for example, the government administrators have devised a program whereby crocodiles are raised in captivity and protected from their natural predators until they are fully grown. About half of each litter is eventually released in the wild, while the other half is sold legally for their skins, with a share of the profits going to the local Maya. With the help of the scientists, local farmers are learning how to better regulate their lobster fishing so as not to deplete the waters of this crustacean, an essential source of income for the community. The friendship between the two groups has also benefited the scientific world, because local shamans are sharing their secrets of herbal medicine with the Sian Ka'an researchers.

The part of Sian Ka'an that is open to tourists is the outer buffer zone. The first 6 miles (10 km) of the drive, as far as Boca Paila, is along the coast and the land is fairly firm. This is jungle, but far less wild than what lies ahead. Boca Paila, a small community that caters to the whims of elite fly fishermen (accommodations here run about $250 a night per person, double occupancy, with no air conditioning; see *Best en Route*), is set on a tranquil lagoon hemmed in by a mangrove forest. From Boca Paila, hire a boat for fishing or bird watching along the Sian Ka'an coast to the south.

From Boca Paila, the road continues to deteriorate as it winds inward toward the marshy swampland to the south. Because this part of the tour is less traveled than the first leg of the road, you are more likely to catch a glimpse of local reptiles and mammals. Keep an eye peeled for an oversize boa wrapped around a palmy vine or a spotted margay scurrying across the roadway. Iguanas are everywhere and the comical basilisk, rather like a miniature *Tyrannosaurus rex,* can be seen flitting from shrub to shrub in search of a grasshopper meal. Stop the car for a few minutes: You will probably be able to hear the wail of the howler monkey calling to his mate, and there may be a pretty kinkajou, or honey bear, hidden in the branches of a mangrove tree curiously studying your four-wheeled beast. Closer to Punta Allen, a hazy mist encircles the forests. The barren tops of dead coconut trees tower above the all-consuming fog like mammoth shafts in a hauntingly beautiful twilight zone landscape. It seems the road will never end, when suddenly Punta Allen appears.

PUNTA ALLEN After so many miles of wilderness, the modest playground and basketball court at the entrance to Punta Allen are an abrupt, but most welcome, promise of civilization.

There are several guides available for boat trips into the placid Bay of Ascención, home to most of Mexico's manatee and dolphin population. There is also an island called Cayo Culebras, inhabited by several colonies of frigate birds. Also known as man-o'-war birds, the frigates have the longest wingspan of any sea bird. During the winter months, the male frigate displays a bright red gular pouch which balloons to almost 30% of his normal size. It is an astounding vision right out of the pages of *National Geographic* magazine. Fly fishermen will find the waters around the island literally jumping with barracuda, tarpon, red drum, snook, pompano, bluefish, and wahoo. Fishing in and around Sian Ka'an is on a catch-and-release basis only, but a local photographer is always on hand to provide documentation of your angling talents.

For a slightly higher fee, hire a canoe and travel through a series of connecting lagoons to the unexplored Chunyaaxché ruins, which date back 20,000 years. (For rental information, ask Sonia López, owner of the *Cuzan* guesthouse in Punta Allen.)

Almost all the dining facilities are rustic at Punta Allen, and lobster tail is a staple. Those who spend the night will probably wake to a breakfast of scrambled eggs and lobster — pretty fancy fare for roughing it. To resume the route to Chetumal, retrace your steps on the unnumbered road back to Tulum and Route 307.

En route to Chetumal From here, the highway south bends westward and inland 146 miles (243 km), until it dead-ends with Route 186 along the Belize border. To the west, Route 186 continues through the jungle for 159 miles (254 km), to meet up eventually with the town of Escárcega and then doubles back north as Route 261, completing the Yucatán loop. This is a lonely, deserted highway with little to offer save steamy vegetation and a generous portion of potholes. To the east, Route 186 leads 12 miles (19 km) straight into Chetumal. There will be plenty of signs indicating which way to turn.

FELIPE CARRILLO PUERTO The first town of any significant size on the road from Tulum is Felipe Carrillo Puerto, 59 miles (94 km) south of the ancient walled city. This town gets its name from a populist Yucatán governor of the 1920s; the town has little to recommend it except for an extraordinary restaurant on the highway called *El Faisán y El Venado* (The Pheasant and the Deer), which serves fresh venison steaks perfectly prepared at extremely reasonable prices. You won't find it on the menu, because technically commercial deer hunting is *verboten* in Quintana Roo, but the restaurant is a town tradition and local authorities turn a blind eye to the sale of venison in exchange for a discount price on a meal. Ask your waiter for *venado* (venison), in a low voice as discreetly as possible.

Continue south on Route 307 about 70 miles (112 km) to Bacalar Lagoon.

LAGUNA DE BACALAR The crystalline "Lake of Seven Colors" is the place where the ancient Maya thought the rainbow was born. Those who witness the red, turquoise, blue, and violet tones that this magnificent natural wonder reflects throughout the day can easily understand the reasons for this belief. Surrounded by a wall of gently sloped hills, the lagoon's waters are so still that at times they seem like a mirror of brightly polished glass. This is a perfect setting for boating, swimming, or snorkeling, and there are two very pleasant hotels along the shore, *La Laguna* and *Rancho Encantado* (see *Best en Route*), for those who want to spend the night and watch the sunrise on the lagoon.

Although the main reason for stopping off in Bacalar is the lagoon, the town has a bonus attraction that is often overlooked: San Felipe, a stately stone fort constructed by Spanish colonists during the first half of the 18th century.

Founded in 1528 (14 years before Mérida), Villa Real (Royal Village), as Bacalar was originally called, was the first major Spanish outpost on the Yucatán Peninsula. Unable to subdue the fierce and primitive Maya in Chetumal, conquistador Alfonso Dávila decided to establish a military base along the lagoon to regroup his forces for an attack. The post was poorly protected and could easily have been overpowered by the Maya warriors, but rather than waste his men and energy storming the colonial encampment, the chieftain of Chetumal decided to bide his time and let the elements of nature conquer the conquerors. Within 2 years, disease, mosquitoes, and the stifling heat of the jungle had bested the Spanish army, and Villa Real was abandoned.

Fifteen years later, the Spanish made a second attempt to settle the area, this time under the capable direction of Melchor Pacheco, who repopulated the fort and dubbed it "Nueva Salamanca de Bacalar" (New Salamanca of Bacalar), in honor of his hometown. The new colonists were better prepared for their stay in the wilderness: They transported their ample supplies — brought from the Old World — through a canal they had dug linking the lagoon to the Caribbean Sea. The colonists survived for almost a century in relative peace. But by 1640, Spanish-Maya tensions were aggravated by the brutal murders of four local farmers, and the Chetumal community stormed the settlement in retaliation. For well over 2 years, the bloodletting continued, and almost 75% of the Spanish colonists were killed or fled. Those who stayed became easy prey for pirates and English corsairs, who razed Bacalar in 1652. Exasperated, the Spanish government decided it was high time to gird its interests in the southern Yucatán. In 1725, Antonio Figueroa y Silva, governor of the peninsula, ordered the transportation of the entire Spanish population of the Canary Islands to Bacalar in order to construct a massive fortress to defend the town. The 30-foot-high structure took 25 years to complete, but although its 4-towered walls and 12-foot-deep crocodile-laden moat were impressive to look at, they were militarily weak against attack. Still, the San Felipe Fort served its purpose, inhibiting the number of raids by outside intruders. The town prospered from its chicle and coconut plantations, and by 1847 a road was constructed that linked Bacalar to Mérida through the southern jungles.

Had the Castes War not broken out in 1848, the city probably would be the capital of Quintana Roo today. But once again, the Chetumal Maya released their fury on the people of Bacalar, and after a bitter struggle San Felipe fell into Maya hands. The British in Belize, happy to see the Spanish overcome in a region they considered rightfully theirs, actually recognized Venancío Pec, the Maya military head, as the official governor of the city, a move that infuriated the Spanish and led to quick annihilation of Pec and his army. Once the Spanish had regained face, they abandoned the city and the Maya timidly reclaimed it, this time without any vainglorious shows of victory. For 50 years, Bacalar was a Maya city. It was not until 1901 that the Mexican government finally decided to peacefully repossess the fort and its surroundings, in order to use it as a commercial stopover between Felipe Carrillo Puerto and Chetumal.

San Felipe Fort, now a museum which houses old weapons, artifacts, and a magnificent mural, is open to the public from 9 AM to 6 PM daily. A park of well-manicured gardens surrounds the 150-square-foot fortress. The central watchtower offers a scenic view of the town and lagoon. Admission charge.

CENOTE AZUL This azure cenote (sinkhole), just 3 miles (5 km) south of Bacalar on Route 307, is a perfect place for a dip in the water, Maya-style. The limestone pool of sweet water is 600 feet wide and almost 280 feet deep and is surrounded by eucalyptus and other shade trees. The small, rustic, open-air *Cenote Azul* restaurant, on the banks, serves fresh fish and other seafood. The house specialty is an excellent dish of giant shrimp stuffed with cheese, wrapped in bacon, and deep-fried. There are also camping facilities nearby for those who want to spend the night under the stars; open from 10 AM to 6 PM daily.

Follow Route 307 south 12 miles (19 km) to the junction with Route 186 along the Belize border; turn east here on Route 186 for 14 miles (23 km) to Chetumal.

CHETUMAL Originally a Maya city, Chetumal or *Chetemal* ("Place of the Falling Rain") was inhabited in 2000 BC, making it one of the oldest cities on the Yucatán Peninsula. Its strategic location on the Bay of San José and the mouth of the Hondo River has always made it a sought-after military and commercial base. When the Spaniards landed on the peninsula in the early 1500s, they tried to subdue the natives of Chetumal and claim the location for their own, but the Maya had other ideas. After a futile battle that lasted nearly 3 weeks, the Spanish armies packed up their gear and retreated north to Bacalar Lagoon. The conquistadores then tried to sweet-talk the Maya into surrendering Chetumal, this time offering them trinkets, baubles, and other European "riches" in barter; but again the Maya refused to yield. The third attempt by the Spanish was clearly a might-is-right approach: In 1544, storming the Maya city at night with 12 battalions of rifled soldiers and savage attack dogs, the Spaniards finally brought the Maya (at least temporarily) to their knees. This assault was to go down as one of the most barbaric and cruel in the annals of Mexican history. Women and children, even newborn babies, were dismembered or chained to stones and cast into the ocean screaming for mercy. Turning a deaf ear, the Spaniards pillaged the city. There were even accounts of macabre mutilations and cannibalism on the part of the conquerors. The few Maya who did survive either escaped into the jungle or were left to starve to death amid the plundered ruins.

Under Spanish dominion, Chetumal thrived. Copra, cocoa, and banana plantations as well as lumber and sugar mills prospered, and for about 50 years Chetumal was an exemplary colonial city. But the long memory and simmering wrath of the Maya knew no absolution, and in a lightning attack in the summer of 1583, the city fell back into native hands as quickly as it had been lost almost half a century before. The Spanish-Maya struggle to take and hold the coveted city went on for 3 centuries, with the lengthy tally of casualties mounting with every battle. Only in 1898 did the Maya finally lose their tenacious grasp on the region; Chetumal was declared a Spanish municipality and renamed Payo Obispo (The Peasant Bishop), after a well-known Catholic missionary. At long last the tragic fate of the Chetumal Maya had been sealed. No more would their chieftains rally to combat the white intruders. Chetumal and the southern tip of Quintana Roo were now a conquered land. Eventually, Chetumal would reclaim its original appellation, but the city would never again be a Maya domain.

But what the Maya could not accomplish, nature did. In 1955, Hurricane Janet leveled all but 14 buildings of the teeming border town. Chetumal had to be rebuilt from scratch, this time with financial support from the Mexican government. Modern cement and mortar structures replaced the traditional wood-paneled cottages that had become synonymous with the city. The highway linking the city with Campeche and Mérida made the free-port status of Chetumal big business for importers and traders of legal and illegal goods. Cantinas and houses of ill repute abounded, and Chetumal entered a new heyday of commercial activity.

Today, Chetumal resembles the setting for a stereotypical 1940s Hollywood private-eye story. Balanced delicately on the Mexican border with Belize (formally British Honduras), it still maintains free-port status, impervious to Mexican import tariffs and quotas. This odd little state capital is aglitter with shops selling Japanese electronic devices, Dutch cheeses, Czech crystal, Italian silk, and French perfume. Mexicans usually have to pay 100% (or more) duty on luxury goods from abroad (if the items are allowed into the country at all); so for the people of cities such as Mérida and Villahermosa, Chetumal is the next best thing to Hong Kong. However, with Canada and the US planning to eliminate these protective tariffs, the city's duty-free status is expected to change. Chetumal is also a staging point for hunting and fishing expeditions. Just a mile off shore is the small island of Tamalcab, home of the *tepezcuintles,* small dog-like rodents that are a favorite with hunters.

Unless you have spent the night in Bacalar, you probably will arrive in Chetumal late in the day, which will give you enough time to stroll around town, have dinner, and get a good night's sleep. Formal, numbered street addresses are rarely used here; like many of the towns in the Yucatán, Chetumal is small and easy to negotiate, and shops, restaurants, and hotels simply don't use addresses.

Payo Obispo Zoo has specimens of indigenous wildlife, including the manatee and the kinkajou, as well as a small museum featuring exhibits recounting the city's tormented history and a few artifacts from Kohunlich. Closed Mondays. Admission charge. Av. Insurgentes on the corner of Andrés Roo.

La Cascada at the *Continental Caribe* hotel serves a good selection of seafood and international dishes. If you prefer Italian food, try *Sergio's Pizza,* just off the main boulevard. Late-night snackers will appreciate *24-Horas,* open around the clock, on the main drag. The hotels in Chetumal are comfortable, but nothing to write home about (see *Best en Route*).

From Chetumal, visitors can make a side trip to the Maya vestiges at Kohunlich, 36 miles (58 km) due west on Route 186, toward the town of Escárcega.

KOHUNLICH Officially, Kohunlich was discovered in 1967, when construction workers came upon the ruins while cutting a *trocha,* or path, for Route 186. Like all the other Maya cities, Kohunlich is a former ceremonial center, or temple. Its pyramids were observatories from which the seasons were measured. In the tropics, where winter blends into spring with no robins to herald the change, spotting the equinox was a great problem and of vital importance to the Maya, for it told them when to plant their corn. It is probable that only the high priests, who lived in the temples and performed rites on top of the pyramids, knew how to differentiate the seasons. Because the area has only recently begun to be excavated, most of Kohunlich is as yet undiscovered. You can best appreciate the vast size of this city from a vantage-point view atop its Pyramid of the Masks. Archaeologists have determined that this pyramid contained tombs; the only other Maya pyramids known to have been used as burial places are at Altun Ha (see below) and at Palenque (in the nearby state of Chiapas).

Four temples stand at Kohunlich, along with a plaza of large stone bas-relief plaques and the ubiquitous ball court, where the Maya played a game that appears to have been a combination of modern-day soccer and basketball. The idea was to get a hard rubber ball through the opposing team's goal, which was a small stone ring. Players were not allowed to use their hands to score. Considering the small circumference of the goal ring, this must have been quite difficult. The teams did their best, however, and according to legend, the victory was celebrated with the decapitation (considered a noble death) of the winning team's captain, symbolically fertilizing the ground with his blood.

Kohunlich is by no means as well ordered as Uxmal (see *The Yucatán Peninsula: Cancún to Campeche,* in this section). Archaeologists continue to look for clues as to how the Maya lived and why the civilization disappeared. Visitors may well get a sense of ongoing exploration and feel as if they actually are in the midst of potentially important discoveries. The grounds are extremely beautiful, and the lush carpet of green grass and thick jungle that frame the site give it a mystical quality unlike the more commonly visited ruins of Tulum, Cobá, and Chichén Itzá. If you go, be sure to take insect repellent, because Kohunlich is home to the biggest, meanest mosquitoes in the peninsula, and the welts from their bites can last a week.

Retrace Route 186 back to Chetumal.

If time permits, the British Commonwealth Republic of Belize, just south of Chetumal, offers a delightful change of pace from standard Mexican meanderings. For more information on this small country and its distinctively colonial appeal, pick up a copy of *Birnbaum's Caribbean 1994,* edited by Alexandra Mayes Birnbaum (HarperCollins: $18).

BEST EN ROUTE

The available accommodations along the route are, with few exceptions, far less posh than those found on more traditional tourist trails. The quality of service is also not always up to par with international standards, but for the most part, neither are the prices. Many of the places below are rustic to an extreme — you may end up sleeping in a hammock instead of a bed — but they all are usually clean and as close to topnotch as you can get in this region. Most of them do not have phones or fax machines to handle reservations, but they will almost always manage to accommodate drop-ins. The big exception to this rule is in Boca Paila, where reservations are recommended for the often pricey accommodations. The up side of these slight inconveniences is that there is a homey feeling at most places, and they will often go that extra mile to please their guests. Breakfast is sometimes included in the price, and the wholesome goodness of Mexican cooking can be a welcome relief from industrialized commercial kitchens. If prices inside the confines of Sian Ka'an seem high, the reason is that everything here must be brought in from outside. Also, there is no public electricity in the biosphere, so individual generators must be used to provide light and energy. For a double room, expect to pay up to $250 at an expensive hotel; $40 to $90 in moderate places; and $35 and under in inexpensive ones.

COBÁ

Villa Arquecaológica Run by Club Med, it's the only hotel at the ruins in Cobá, and is set in an isolated jungle environment close to many unexplored sites. You actually can get out of bed and hack your way through the jungle. There are 40 units, tennis courts, a swimming pool, and a library on Mesoamerican archaeology (phone: 5-203-3086 or 5-203-3833 in Mexico City; 800-CLUB-MED in the US). Moderate.

BOCA PAILA

Club de Pesca Boca Paila This rustic little lodge has 6 cabins with no air conditioning, no TV sets, and no other amenities to speak of. What it does offer is superb saltwater fly fishing. This rusticity doesn't come cheap: $250 per person per night/double occupancy. Don't try to visit without a reservation; the place is booked months in advance, and there is a house policy not to receive drop-ins. (phone: 987-20053 or 987-20124; 800-245-1950 in the US). Expensive.

Pez Maya From the same folks who brought you *Club de Pesca Boca Paila* comes this set of 7 cabins at an even higher price — stripped bare (and we do mean bare!) of the usual necessities and with little else to offer but fly fishing (phone: 987-20072). Expensive.

PUNTA ALLEN

Posada Cuzan This modest collection of thatch tepees is run by an American who believes that a taste of nature is worth a little discomfort. The rooms are clean, but you may end up having to sleep in a hammock, because there are only a few beds. The dining room, a huge cabaña with a sand floor, serves exceptionally good food (fax: 983-40383 in Felipe Carrillo Puerto). Inexpensive.

BACALAR

Rancho Encantado A cozy, lakeside, 5-cottage resort, its restaurant has a continental menu. Lots of personal touches show the interest of the American-born owners. The gardens are wonderful for leisurely strolls under the orchid-laden palms that line Bacalar Lagoon. Worth an extra day's layover. Reservations essential. Rte. 307 just north of Bacalar City (phone: 983-80427; 800-221-0555 in the US). Expensive.

La Laguna This is a clean, family-run, 34-unit establishment with air conditioning, a swimming pool, a restaurant — and some of the slowest service on the face of the earth. That notwithstanding, the view of the lagoon is spectacular, and there is a small boat dock. 316 Bugambilias (phone: 983-23517). Moderate.

CHETUMAL

Continental Caribe This first class hotel has air conditioned rooms, a swimming pool, a bar, a restaurant, a garage, and movies (with English subtitles). 171 Av. Héroes (phone: 983-21100). Expensive.

Del Prado Run by one of Mexico's largest hotel chains, with 76 air conditioned rooms, a swimming pool, a restaurant, and a bar, this is by far the best in town. Héroes del Chapultepec (phone: 983-20544; 800-STAYMEX in the US). Expensive.

Aztec A pleasant place, with air conditioned units, parking, a restaurant, and a bar. 186 Belice (phone: 983-20666). Moderate.

Jacaranda Clean and comfortable, this unforgettable bargain glows with an old colonial, outpost-of-empire atmosphere. 201 Alvaro Obregón (phone: 983-21455). Moderate.

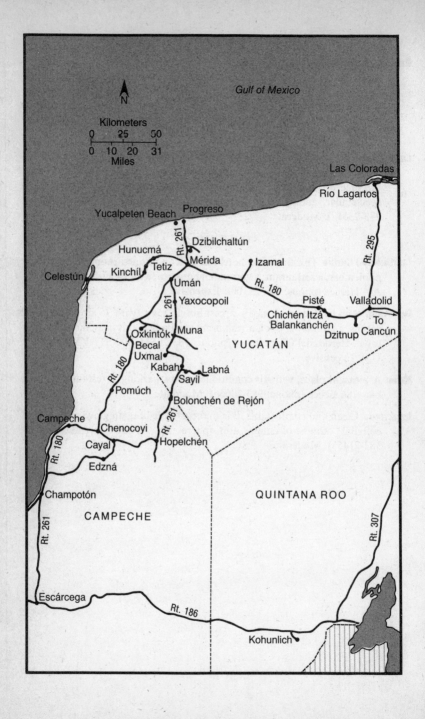

The Yucatán Peninsula: Cancún to Campeche

The Yucatán Peninsula encompasses the three Mexican states — Yucatán, Campeche, and Quintana Roo — that jut into the Gulf of Mexico where it joins the Caribbean Sea. Most famous for the magnificent Maya ruins at Chichén Itzá, the Yucatán also has a walled city that could have come right out of a late-show pirate movie, outposts of an empire that Graham Greene might have invented, and some of the most enchanting resorts in the entire Caribbean, the best-known being the islands of Cancún, Cozumel, and Isla Mujeres. While Isla Mujeres and Cozumel, the largest island in all of Mexico, have no land connecting them with the mainland, Cancún is linked to the peninsula by two long, sandy causeways built in the 1970s (see *Mexico's Caribbean Coast: Cancún to Tulum,* in this section).

The state where these islands are located is Quintana Roo (pronounced Kin-tah-nah *Row*), the youngest in the Mexican republic (along with Baja California Sur, it was given full autonomy in 1974). The state — which takes its name from Andrés Quintana Roo, a hero in Mexico's War of Independence — was originally part of the state of Yucatán but was lopped off in reprisal for the Yucatecans' rebellious ways. Until recently, the *yucatecos* considered that no great loss. Once the former federal territory was granted statehood, however, the Yucatán state created a boundary dispute. Considering that the border runs through still unexplored jungle, no one has taken the *yucatecos* challenge very seriously to date, but with the growing development of tourism throughout the region, it seems likely that the issue will come to a political head within the course of the next few years, and formal boundary lines will no doubt be established.

In many ways, the three states on the peninsula constitute a country within a country. While the rest of the mainland is made up of hills, forests, and deserts originally settled by the Aztec, the peninsula consists of the flat jungles of the Maya. About the size of Arizona, the peninsula was isolated from the rest of Mexico for centuries. Mainland Mexicans may joke about the Yucatán as a "sister republic," but several times in the course of its history the peninsula has in fact almost become a separate country. During the 19th century especially, there were more than a few efforts at secession. When these failed, the Yucatecans responded by and large by simply ignoring the government in Mexico City, pretending as best they could that it didn't exist.

The Maya came from Central America to settle in the Yucatán about 500 BC, around the same time that the ancient Greek civilization was flourishing. The Maya, in fact, had more in common with the Greeks than just contemporaneity. Like the Greeks', theirs was a civilization more intellectual than political; and like the Greeks, they never managed to form any kind of unified national political organization. Each Maya city was a little kingdom unto itself. And for some reason as yet undiscovered, one after another the great cities of the Maya — really ceremonial centers — were abandoned. Though a number of theories have been put forward to try to explain this, no one really knows why. During the 11th century, just about the time the Normans were conquering England, the Toltec conquered the Maya. The Toltec were from central Mexico and had a culture similar in many ways to that of the Aztec, who later became the most successful and powerful tribe in pre-Spanish Mexico.

Two large mysteries remain unexplained about the Maya before the Toltec invasion: why they moved from Central America into the Yucatán Peninsula in the first place, and why they periodically abandoned the magnificent ceremonial cities they built at various sites around the jungle peninsula. The answer to both questions is most likely buried in the glyphs (pictographs etched into stone) found at Chichén Itzá and other ruins, but these have not been fully deciphered. It's thought that the long messages carved into the giant ruins contain information about the Maya god-kings' ancestors, their lives and deaths, rituals and relationships. The spoken language of the Maya, on the other hand, is very much alive. The chatter in any market in the Yucatán is more likely to be in Maya than in Spanish.

The Toltec invaded the Yucatán after they had been driven out of the central highlands near the Valley of Mexico, where the Aztec, that roaming and warlike group of Indians, eventually settled. The Toltec brought to the Yucatán the worship of the plumed serpent, Quetzalcóatl, whom the Maya called Kukulcán. The serpent was the symbol of a god whose other identities included those of a priest and a king. The founder of the Toltec capital of Tula took Quetzalcóatl's name as his own and assumed the position of high priest to the god. According to legend, Quetzalcóatl populated the world by pouring his blood over the bones of people who had died from an earlier world; this myth of a god nurturing mankind with his own blood became the basis of ritual sacrifice, which the Toltec brought to the Yucatán.

Interestingly, the Maya absorbed the Toltec as much as the Toltec influenced Maya theology and building; many of the ruins show Toltec forms. Essentially the Toltec became latter-day Maya.

Although the Maya lands were occupied, the Maya could claim with some justification that they were never really conquered. The first Europeans to arrive were immediately chased away. The Yucatán was finally breached by Europeans in 1517, with a brief visit by Francisco Hernández de Córdoba. Spanish conquistador Juan de Grijalva renamed the region

New Spain in 1518. Hernán Cortés explored the coast, landed in 1519, and soon was greeted by Aztec emissaries from central Mexico, who believed he was the fair-skinned Quetzalcóatl, returning as predicted in legend. Cortés's march to the Aztec capital at Tenochtitlán started in 1519 in Veracruz, which he founded. Twenty years after the Halls of Montezuma had been sledged into rubble, Francisco de Montejo founded Mérida in the western Yucatán. The surrounding area never completely fell under Spanish domination, and Mexico's independence in 1821 did little to change things. The Castes War, in which remnants of the Maya battled outside domination, dragged on through most of the 19th century.

Eventually, economics did what force of arms could not. The production of *henequén,* a form of sisal used in making rope, changed the economic and social systems in the Yucatán. The US and European nations needed rope for their ships. The Yucatán was a handy source of supply, and the great *henequén* plantations began to thrive. A feudal system of land ownership developed, and the Yucatán Indians became peons on great Spanish haciendas. The hacienda owners, for their part, discovered wealth beyond their avaricious dreams. Like the rich of many other lands, they turned toward Europe for cultural standards and status. They sent their children to schools on the Continent or, when they could not get to Paris themselves, settled for New Orleans. The owners of the haciendas were very similar to their counterparts in Peru, who allowed Indians to work the land while they partied in Paris rather than journey into the interior of their own country. The Yucatán *hacendados,* the landowners, ignored the rest of Mexico partly because, before the air age, it was difficult to reach and partly because, as far as the aristocracy was concerned, it was not worth the effort.

Today, a highway system completely circles the peninsula, and driving is the best way to get a feeling for the entirety of this magnificent area — from the resort area of Cancún on the Caribbean to the inland routes to Mérida, passing Chichén Itzá and other major archaeological areas. This route can be completed in 4 easy days of driving, seldom with more than 6 hours spent on a road in any single given day. But there's so much to see that for an in-depth look, even a week is sometimes not enough. All in all the roads are good, the countryside flat, and destinations fairly close to each other.

The Yucatán today is still vastly different from the rest of Mexico. The *yucateco* accent is as distinct as a Southern drawl in the US. To this day, *henequén* remains the major crop and can be seen growing in expansive fields along the highways. In the villages, people still speak Maya, live in white, oval, thatch huts called *chozas,* and wear white garments — embroidered *huipiles* for women, tailored *guayaberas* for the men. Almost nowhere else in Mexico are native costumes seen with such frequency as in the Yucatán. The peninsula has its own cuisine, too. Pork *pibil* is one of the favorite dishes, while venison and pheasant are still basic staples in the local diet. Yucatán beer and ale, particularly the Montejo brand of stout, rare outside the immediate region, are prized throughout Mexico. Teetotalers will want to sample *soldado* (soldier), a local chocolate-flavored soft drink, available across the peninsula.

While the glitzy polish of Cancún and the raw beauty of the Yucatán's untamed jungles have much to offer, they are hardly representative samples of what Mexico is all about. The states of Yucatán and Campeche reflect a colonial heritage of grace and elegance in stately mansions and staid cathedrals. The archaeological ruins in these states are also better restored and far more accessible to the public; its citizens have family roots dating back several centuries, and are proud of their ancestral home. This attitude is clearly echoed in the warmth and hospitality they extend to visitors.

Interestingly, the name "Yucatán" comes from a rather humorous misunderstanding. When the Spaniards first landed in the region in the early 1500s, they asked the indigenous Maya what the area was called. Confused, the Indians replied in their native tongue, *"Ci u than,"* which meant "We don't understand you." Somehow the Spaniards transmogrified the Maya phrase and officially dubbed the territory Yucatán.

Hitting the Yucatán trail inevitably means a trip to Chichén Itzá and at least 1 night's stay in Mérida, but those with more time will want to extend their explorations. To the south lie the stunning ruins of Uxmal and the "forgotten" state of the Yucatán trilogy, Campeche, offering seclusion, sensational seafood, and a fortress from pirate days. To the north is the newly renovated port city of Progreso. To the west, there's the breathtaking flamingo refuge of Celestún. In short, the Yucatán has something for every taste.

En route from Cancún The highway from Cancún to Mérida is Route 180, a 201-mile (322-km) trip which will take at least 4 hours to drive, not counting time out to visit the ruins of Chichén Itzá or any of the other sights along the way. Count on spending at least 1 night in Mérida, although with so much to see in the Yucatán, you will probably want to stay as long as your itinerary will allow. To continue on to Campeche, add at least 1 more day to your agenda. A side trip to Celestún or Progreso, or a diversion to Río Lagartos, will mean still another day's drive. Mérida itself is worth spending time in. This colonial city has a traditional charm and distinctive character not found in the flashy resorts of Quintana Roo. The center of colonial Yucatán, Mérida is still the largest city on the peninsula, and the focus of all major business. This is the real Mexico, not a tinsel-town showcase built to appease sun worshipers and party animals. History radiates from every street corner, and the warmth of Yucatecan hospitality is reflected in the smiles of everyone you meet.

The road from Cancún to the border between Quintana Roo and the state of Yucatán is chock-full of enough potholes to make a visitor want to turn around and go back, but take heart: Once you get past the border checkpoint at Pueblo Nuevo, 55 miles (88 km) down the so-called highway, the driving conditions improve 100% There will still be a bounty of obstacles on the road, but they will be in the form of speed bumps, intentionally placed and adequately marked in advance. Chichén Itzá, the most famous of the Maya ruins, lies 71 miles (114 km) farther. If time permits, visit Valladolid, about 41 miles (66 km) west of Pueblo Nuevo on Route 180, a large city with some lovely colonial buildings and a 16th-century Franciscan monastery in the center of town.

Take Route 295 north from Valladolid for 65 miles (104 km) to Río Lagartos.

RÍO LAGARTOS Although it is certainly a major deviation from the route to Mérida, a side trip to Río Lagartos is a must for nature lovers. On the northernmost coast of the Yucatán state, this national wildlife reserve is one of only three known nesting grounds for flamingos in the world. Surrounded by dense tropical jungles, this flat, marshy cluster of lagoons is covered every May and June with literally thousands of salmon-hued flamingos that come to lay their eggs and nurture their young. The nesting ground is a peculiar sight to behold. Muddy, cone-shape nests, each accommodating only a single egg, protrude like giant anthills from the marshy waters. The female flamingos stand watch at one end of the nests, gracefully balancing themselves on one leg. Depending on the time of year (although spring is their nesting season), there is usually also a colony of white fledglings (they don't turn pink until they are at least 3 months old). During the spring incubation period, it's hard to get close to the flamingos. Protective of their nests, they startle more easily than usual and if disturbed, panic and often destroy their own eggs. If you do go during the nesting season, your guide will no doubt discourage any attempt to approach the colony any nearer than 100 yards. Throughout the rest of the year, it is possible to get within 70 to 80 yards of the birds without their flying away.

There are several ways to track the flamingos in Río Lagartos, the most practical being on a rented boat captained by a local guide (don't worry about finding a guide; they seem to be everywhere, eager to shepherd visitors through the area). More adventurous flamingo stalkers will want to hike out to the breeding grounds. This can be a tedious and time-consuming experience, but true nature enthusiasts will find it to their liking to explore the abandoned mangrove marshes at the same time that they are hunting the ruby-colored avifauna. Those who opt to go by foot should be sure to wear rubber-soled shoes and take along insect repellent. Though there are several types of water snakes in the area, none are poisonous. Still, it's a good idea to plan to be back in the local town way before dark. It's easy to get lost in the mangroves at night, and although most of the crocodile population that gave the reserve its name (*lagartos* is Spanish for lizards) have been killed off over the years by illegal hunters, you wouldn't want to have a close encounter with one of the few surviving specimens.

Since it will take at least 2 to 3 hours, even by boat, to reach the nesting grounds, you will most likely want to spend the night in the town's only hotel geared for tourists, the *Nefertiti* (see *Best en Route*) — but don't expect the *Ritz*.

DZITNUP Retrace the drive on Route 295 to Route 180 toward Mérida; just 3 miles (5 km) west of Valladolid, is a sign for Dzitnup (pronounced *Tsit*-nupe). If you are in the mood for a geologic excursion, this town is 2 miles (3 km) off the main road and boasts what many consider to be the most beautiful cenote (sinkhole) in the Yucatán state.

The entire village (almost exclusively inhabited by Maya descendants) is built around the cenote, very much the way it must have been in pre-Columbian times. With a diameter of nearly 100 yards, the cenote is an almost perfect circle surrounded by the high stone walls of a cave that collapsed millions of years ago. There are now some roughly carved steps leading down to the transparent, shallow waters, which are thick with tropical foliage and water lilies.

The sinkhole itself is called Xkekén (pronounced Shke-*ken*), which translates loosely to "light from the earth," referring to the incandescent shade of turquoise that reflects on the clear water. In fact, the light is filtered through a giant natural skylight created by the collapsed walls of the cavern. But by some geologic quirk, the light seems to come from below ground, giving the place an eerie, almost supernatural feeling.

The water is fresh and inviting. There are schools of an extraordinary speckled blind fish (which evolved in the dark caves) that tend to congregate around the edge of the cenote. This unusual species is unique to the Yucatán Peninsula, and is currently being studied by the Mexican National Fisheries Institute.

CHICHÉN ITZÁ About 29 miles (46 km) further west on Route 180 is Chichén Itzá. The site, spanning two great eras of Maya civilization, offers fine examples of Classic and Post-Classic architectural styles with a powerful Toltec influence.

Some of the most dramatic ruins in all of Mexico, these cover 7 square miles. Plumed serpents, carved in stone, appear everywhere in this place, whose name means "at the mouth of the well of the Itzá" (a Maya tribe).

The Toltec built structures in their own style, exemplified at Tula; good examples here are the Temple of the Warriors, the Group of a Thousand Columns, the Temple of Kukulcán, the Temple of the Chac-Mool, and the ball court.

Part of Chichén Itzá, the "new" city, lies on one side of the highway, surrounding El Castillo (The Castle) Pyramid; the ball court (with acoustics so fine a voice scarcely louder than a whisper can be heard 500 feet away); the Temple of the Jaguars, dedicated to an order of warriors; the

Temple of the Eagles and the Tigers; and the Thousand Columns (probably the marketplace), with pillars resembling plumed serpents that at one time, no doubt, supported a roof. Here and there are the Chac-Mools, reclining idols that in spite of their name are no relation to Chac, the rain god. Chac-Mools were the centerpiece on sacrificial altars. They held large bowls in which were placed the still-beating human hearts torn from living victims. Less gory but equally tragic is the sacrificial well, the large cenote lying a short walk from the other ruins. Its depths have been extensively explored, but archaeologists have recovered only a fraction of its contents. The bottom is a bramble of branches and twigs. Recently, divers have brought up the bones of the victims — men, women, and even children. Youngsters were considered most precious; hence, they were the greatest treasure that could be offered to the rain god.

The Toltec initiated rites of human sacrifice at Chichén Itzá. The zompantli (a platform on which human skulls were exhibited) is decorated with carved stone skulls, and the ball court displays carved relief figures depicting the traditional sacrificial death of the winning team's captain (considered a great honor by the Toltec).

The Temple of Kukulcán displays a mixture of architectural features — Toltec warrior reliefs as well as Maya corbeled vaults. At the topmost altar, reached by an interior stairway, is a stone statue of a jaguar, painted red with jade eyes and spots and white flint fangs still in place.

Sculptures of Toltec warriors are carved on the columns of the Temple of the Warriors. Chac-Mools, feathered serpents, and small Atlantean figures recall the style of Tula. Murals recount the story of battles between this tribe and surrounding groups. In the Temple of the Chac-Mool, paintings on the benches show Toltec seated on jaguar thrones and Maya rulers on jaguar skin–covered stools.

The ruins of Old Chichén across the road are rather less impressive. There is another cenote, or sinkhole well, but it was used for more peaceful purposes, as a water supply. A round observatory, El Caracol (The Snail), in Old Chichén gets its name from the spiral stairway within; its circular structure makes it a rarity among Maya buildings. Some of the observatory's features resemble El Castillo Pyramid. The windows are aligned in such a way as to record the longest and shortest days of the year and are set to permit measurement of astronomical phenomena with precision. On the first day of spring and the first day of autumn, shadows form a serpent's body leading from the temple on top to the carved head on the bottom.

Also in the group of ruins is the ossuary, or bone depository, a 30-foot-high pyramid with stairways on each side and a miniature temple on top. The temple is in the same form as El Castillo Pyramid. This building was used by the Toltec as a burial place. Nearby is the Akad-Dzib, a building of obscure writings and red handprints believed to have something to do with Kabul or Zamná, the god whose name meant "heavenly hand."

There is a smaller group of buildings in Old Chichén that are still overgrown with jungle vegetation. You have to walk along some rough trails to get to them. The structures in this part of Chichén Itzá include the Castillo of Old Chichén, the Temple of the Turtle, the Temple of the Sculptured Jambs, the Temples of the Lintels, and the Temple of the Hieroglyphic Jambs. The paths leading among the different temples are known as *sacbes,* or holy paths, where people often were led to be ultimately sacrificed. There's a sound-and-light show with English narration at 9 PM. Closed Mondays. Admission charge.

In the nearby town of Pisté is *Xaybé,* a large, airy restaurant with leather-strung chairs and a handsome wrought-iron mural; it offers attentive service and a fixed-price (inexpensive) menu that includes good broiled pork chops and baked chicken. There are also buffets for large groups and a generous selection of mixed drinks (phone: 985-62462).

BALANKANCHÉN CAVERNS Only 5 miles (8 km) from the ruins at Chichén Itzá lie caves sealed for some 500 years. Their beauty is impressive, and entering them today gives one the feeling of stepping into sacred space; in fact, the local descendants of the Maya, who used to hold ceremonies here, thought carefully before opening the caves to the public. The passageways are narrow and steep, and even small children have to stoop sometimes; those prone to claustrophobia stand forewarned. At the end of the caves is a perfectly clear pool that gives one the impression of peering into a canyon. Groups are limited to a minimum of 3 and a maximum of 15 (oxygen gets scarce fast). Tours, which last 45 minutes, are given by local guides from 9 AM to 4 PM, with a break from noon to 2 PM, or can be arranged through travel agencies in Mérida. Closed Mondays. Admission charge.

IZAMAL About 36 miles (57 km) west of the Balankanchén Caverns on Route 180 is a sign pointing to Izamal. To reach this colonial city, you will have to travel 11 miles (18 km) north on a rather poorly maintained gravel road, but if you are interested in Mexican history, it will be worth the effort. Izamal, also known as the "Yellow City," was once a sacred ceremonial site for the ancient Maya. But when the evangelical Spaniards arrived in 1549, the "pagan" temples were torn down and the stones were used to construct an imposing walled convent and mammoth cathedral. During the colonial period, the city was a thriving center of trade and commerce. But after Mérida became the Yucatán's financial capital in the early 1700s, Izamal practically vanished from the map, falling into a time warp from which it still has not escaped.

There are very few cars to be found here; in fact, the streets are lined with horse-drawn taxis. Most of the 25,000 inhabitants still wear hand-loomed native garments, and inside the church courtyard you will find artisans dipping candles, much the same as they did centuries ago. Incredibly, Izamal has managed to avoid being adulterated by neon lights and billboards. On the down side, though, the city has little to offer in the way of dining or sleeping accommodations.

En route to Mérida Return to Route 180 and continue west 58 miles (93 km) to Mérida.

MÉRIDA (pronounced *May*-ree-dah) The capital of the state of Yucatán and, with a population of 700,000, the only city of significant size on the peninsula (the entire state has barely 1.4 million people), Mérida was founded on January 6, 1542, by Spanish nobleman Don Francisco de Montejo. Having razed the nearby Maya city of T'Ho, Montejo salvaged the debris and quarried the local pyramids for stone to construct a "Christian" settlement in its stead, modeled in the Romanesque style of his birthplace, Mérida, Spain.

The Maya, never a people to be easily conquered, responded to the desecration of their city and holy places with a fierce rebellion against the white intruders. On June 10, 1542, 250 Spaniards held off between 40,000 and 60,000 Maya Indians who attempted to lay siege to Mérida, then only 6 months old. This battle marked the end of the Maya era and the beginning of a feudal land-ownership system in which large tracts of property were owned by the Spanish and worked by the Indians, who toiled virtually as slaves. It wasn't until the 1930s that a more equitable system of distribution gave the Indians of the Yucatán a fairer stake in the land their families had lived on for centuries.

The Maya sites of Chichén Itzá (see above), Uxmal, Sayil, and Kabah are all within driving distance of Mérida, and are among the most remarkable testimonies to a historic civilization anywhere on the American continent — or in the world, for that matter. Still, others visit with no thoughts of archaeology on their minds. Many visitors are nature lovers who come to appreciate the wildlife that inhabit the surrounding natural parks or hunters drawn to the area because of its duck, quail, deer, and wild boar. Indeed, the area has become so popular that some sports enthusiasts make the city the headquarters of their annual or biannual expeditions.

The best source of information about Mérida is your hotel's travel desk or desk clerk, or the tourist information center (in the *Peón Contreras Theater,* Calle 60 near Calle 57; phone: 99-249290); open daily from 8 AM to 8 PM.

Mérida is also something of a tourist destination in its own right. It has its share of interesting colonial buildings, with several good hotels, restaurants, and many shops selling local handicrafts. And it has a distinctive-looking population. Look closely: You will probably notice that quite a few residents have broad faces with high cheekbones, and that their eyes are often almond-shape and their noses somewhat hooked. They are also comparatively short. These are the descendants of the ancient Maya, many of whom speak both Maya and Spanish, or sometimes hardly any Spanish at all — a haunting postscript to any tour of the ruins.

To get a feeling for the city, start at the main plaza, or zocalo, called Plaza de la Independencia: The most interesting sites, shops, hotels, and restaurants are within 3 blocks of the zocalo, and walking is pleasant and easy.

On the south side of the plaza is Casa Montejo, once a lovely Spanish colonial home, built between 1543 and 1549 as the residence for the Montejo family. Now a bank, it is still impressive. The lovely, large rooms were built around two patios and furnished with imported European furniture. Most striking is the stone carving around the entrance door. It's the Montejo coat of arms, flanked on each side by a Spanish conquistador with a foot on the head of a Maya Indian. The figures on top are Adelantado Montejo, his wife, Beatriz, and their daughter, Catalina. Open Mondays through Fridays, 9 AM to 1:30 PM.

Not too far away, on the east side of the zocalo, is the rather majestic, twin-towered cathedral, designed by Juan Miguel de Agüero, the architect who also created Morro Castle in Havana. Above the entrance is the royal coat of arms of Spain; inside, the Chapel of Christ of the Blisters, with a statue reputed to have been carved from the wood of a tree that burned all night but was found untouched the next morning. Open daily, 7 AM to noon and 4 to 8 PM.

Absolutely not to be missed is the Government Palace, on the north side of the plaza at the corner of Calles 60 and 61. Walk into the courtyard and up the back stairs. All the murals lining the walls were painted by Fernando Castro Pacheco, a leading contemporary *yucateco* artist. On the second floor of the building is the Hall of History, easily the handsomest room in all of Mérida. Open daily. No admission charge.

Frequently used for fashionable weddings is the Franciscan Church of the Third Order, located on the east side of Calle 60, at the corner of Calle 59. It is considered by many to be the prettiest church in town.

Four blocks from the plaza, between Calles 66 and 64, La Ermita de Santa Isabel is a tiny church (ca. 1742) notable for its gardens with Maya statuary. Open daily from 8 AM to 11 PM.

As you tour the city, you'll no doubt come upon Paseo Montejo, where wealthy 19th-century residents built splendid homes on a wide, tree-lined imitation Parisian boulevard. An 8-block thoroughfare lined with small palaces, chalets, and extravagant monuments, this is truly one of the most amazing sights in Mexico. Be sure to stop at the Monument to Patriotism, a giant sculpture depicting Mexico's history from the pre-Columbian era to the 20th century.

Refurbished and expanded, *Cantón Palace* (now the *Museum of Anthropology and History*) is one of the finest provincial museums in Mexico. It beautifully depicts the lifestyle of the Maya, and a visit prior to touring the ruins helps bring Maya history into focus. The museum is housed in the *Palacio Cantón,* the largest and perhaps loveliest of the splendid mansions on the Paseo Montejo, formerly the official residence of Yucatán's governors; the entrance is on Calle 43. Closed Mondays. Admission charge.

Once a walled city, Mérida had 13 Moorish gates, of which only 3 remain today. One is the Arco de San Juan (Arch of St. John), about 5 blocks south of the plaza on Calle 64 in San Juan Park, which has a statue of Rachel at the well near its central fountain. This arch leads to the hermitage, La Ermita de Santa Isabel (see above). The Dragon Arch is near the Dragones military regiment's headquarters, at Calles 50 and 61. The third, Bridge Arch, is at Calles 50 and 63.

A bit of a hike from downtown, the *Museo Nacional de Arte Popular* is well worth it. This small museum exhibits masks, pottery, clothing, and other examples of *yucateco* arts and crafts. Upstairs there is an excellent — though completely unorganized — collection of folk art from all over the country. There is also a shop on the first floor, with incredibly reasonable prices. Calle 59 between Calles 48 and 50. Open Tuesdays through Saturdays from 8 AM to 8 PM.. No admission charge.

If you've had your fill (temporarily) of churches, museums, and archaeological tours, Mérida is also a great city for shopping; the public market, or *mercado* (on the corner of Calles 56 and 67), is a good place to find local crafts. It's usually less expensive than any place else in town if you have the patience to bargain. Shops (and offices) usually open between 8 and 9 AM, close for lunch and a siesta from 1 to 4 PM (when the sun is at its strongest), then open again until 8 or 9 PM.

The most popular native crafts are bags and placemats made of sisal, a hemp fiber. Yucatecan hammocks of various sizes, made of fine cotton thread, are a great buy; another is the *jipi,* a fine version of the Panama hat, made by hand near Mérida. The *guayabera,* a tailored men's shirt in solid colors, with or without an embroidered front, is a typical Yucatán product that you can buy in shops throughout Mérida. The average price for a good cotton shirt with long sleeves is less than $25. Most stores also stock a few articles made from tortoiseshell (if purchased, these will be confiscated by US Customs), and there are replicas of the Maya idols. Stores usually have fixed prices, so you can't bargain as in the market. The main shopping streets are Calles 57 and 59 in the 10-block area between Calles 54 and 64.

For sportspeople — spectators and otherwise — Mérida offers a variety of activities. Bullfights are held on Sundays throughout the year, but the big-name matadors usually perform only from January through March. The *Plaza de Toros Mérida* is on Paseo de la Reforma, a block from Avenida Colón.

Good angling can be found at Río Lagartos, famous for the pink flamingos that call it home (see *Río Lagartos*).

Almost all of Mérida's hotels have small swimming pools, and there are quite a few nice beaches and good water skiing 23 miles (37 km) north, at Progreso.

Though Mérida's after-dark action is on the quiet side, the *Calinda Panamericana* has a Mexican fiesta Friday and Saturday evenings and regional dances other nights. *Los Tulipanes* (462 Calle 42; phone: 99-272009) has performances of native and Cuban-style dancing, while the *Montejo Palace* (phone: 99-247644) has a cocktail lounge, and the *Mérida Misión Park Inn* (phone: 99-239500) has a piano bar. The *Trovedor Bohemio* (no phone) and *Peregrina Piano Bar* (by Santa Lucía Park; no phone) both offer drinks and relaxed entertainment, including guitar music. *Kalia Rock House* (no phone), about 10 minutes from downtown, is one of the current favorites. The *Holiday Inn*'s nightclub (phone: 99-256877) is also popular, as are *Oasis, El Cocoon* at the *Calinda Panamericana* (phone: 99-23911), and *Bin Bon Bao* (phone: 99-268752).

Mérida is a good base for those who would like to explore this area but would rather not go through the hassle of packing and unpacking. The following day trips are within easy drives of the city, and the sites can be covered to most travelers' satisfaction within a day's time.

DAY TRIP 1: PROGRESO

Just 23 miles (37 km) to the north of Mérida lies Progreso, the only major seaport on the Yucatán and the peninsula's major commercial link with the outside world since colonial times. Recent expansion offers varied benefits to residents and visitors alike: Today, the city boasts a 2-mile pier, the longest in the world; Route 261 from Mérida to Progreso is the best highway on the peninsula — a well-lighted, meticulously maintained, four-lane thoroughfare; and also on this highway (just 9 miles/14 km north of Mérida, at Km 14 of Route 261) is the state's only golf course, *Club de Golf de Yucatán*. If you didn't bring your clubs, a set can be rented for a small fee (phone: 99-220071 or 99-220053; fax: 99-220054).

DZIBILCHALTÚN (pronounced Zee-bee-chal-*toon*) About 13 miles (21 km) north, just off the road to Progeso, this archaeological site can be reached in about 20 minutes from downtown Mérida. To get there, take Route 261 north 9 miles (14 km), until you reach *Club de Golf de Yucatán* golf course. Turn right and continue down a very narrow road (about one and a half lanes for two-way traffic, so watch out for oncoming vehicles) for about 4 miles (6 km). This archaeological site is believed to have been inhabited longest by the Maya — from about 500 BC until the arrival of the conquistadores. The Temple of the Seven Dolls is especially interesting during the spring and autumn equinoxes, when the light is reflected through parts of this series of complex structures, once used by the Maya as a solar observatory. Open from 8 AM to 5 PM. Closed Mondays. Admission charge.

PROGRESO Back on Route 261, continue north for 14 miles (22 km) beyond *Club de Golf de Yucatán* to Progreso, the hub of the Yucatán's international commercial exchange, where huge crates of honey, cement, sisal rope, fish, steel, and locally assembled lingerie line the docks awaiting dispatch to markets in the US, Canada, and even Europe. There is an electric rail system that transports the cargo to the far end of the pier to be loaded aboard freighters, as well as a wide boulevard open to passenger cars and trucks. It takes a full 5 minutes to drive to the end of the pier, but along the way you can get a feel of the sheer stamina and architectural genius that went into the construction of this engineering feat. The reason the pier is so long is that the Yucatán Peninsula is set on a giant limestone shelf that gradually drops off into the gulf (there are geologic hypotheses that the Yucatán, Cuba, and Florida were once a single expanse of land). For over 3 miles out, the water off the pier is only about 20 feet deep. At the pier's end, there is a visitors' center with a very modern, very clean cafeteria and a small museum which highlights the history of the pier.

In contrast to the turquoise waters of Cancún and Cozumel, the water in the Mexican Gulf is emerald green, and the sand on the beaches is considerably coarser and has a golden hue. The beaches are rarely crowded, and there are water skiing facilities as well as plenty of fishing boats for hire. There is an abundance of open-air fresh seafood restaurants along the shore near the pier, but for a special meal with an Old World flair, drive 10 minutes west along the coastal highway to Yucalpeten Beach and the elegant restaurant at the *Sian-Ka'an* hotel or the equally fine dining place at the *Fiesta Inn* on the *malecón*. These are also ideal spots for an overnight stay for those who want to get away from it all (see *Best en Route*).

After visiting Progreso, take Route 261 south back to Mérida.

DAY TRIP 2: CELESTÚN

Those who didn't get up to Río Lagartos on their way to Mérida still have a chance to view Yucatán flamingos by taking a day trip to Celestún, the state's other major nature reserve. The 58-mile (93-km) drive west on Route 281 is extremely scenic, and the charm of Hunucmá, a quaint little town on the way, is one of the state's best-kept secrets. The drive will take about 2 hours, mainly due to the winding roads, speed bumps, and unexpected obstacles (such as stray cows, lost dogs, and abandoned bicycles) that tend to materialize suddenly in the middle of the highway, so leave early in order to have enough time to see everything. Committed ornithologists may want to spend the night and see these coral-colored birds in the light of dawn. There is a small, very rustic hotel in town which is slightly, albeit *only* slightly, more comfortable than camping out on the beach.

HUNUCMÁ In addition to its exceptional cleanliness, the first thing you will notice about Hunucmá, 18 miles (29 km) west of Mérida, is that all of the houses are fenced by low, whitewashed stone walls. As you follow the meandering road toward the center of town, you will also encounter another distinguishing characteristic of Hunucmá: There are almost no cars, but the streets are teeming with three-wheeled pedicabs busily transporting people, merchandise, and even loads of squeaking piglets from one end of town to the other. These open-air pedaled carriages are an efficient, practical, and inexpensive means of getting around in a town that is spread over 20 square miles of pitted terrain. There is even a central cab rank in the main plaza where pedicabs are ready and waiting to scurry off in any direction a paying passenger may request.

Hunucmá's zocalo, or main square, is also noteworthy. Lined with shady eucalyptus trees, this tranquil plaza, peppered with ice cream carts and *huipil*-clad old women enjoying the afternoon sun, is a scenic vestige of bygone years. On weekends, the plaza comes alive with activity when the local orchestra offers a free concert of Yucatecan music. Across from the plaza stands the 16th-century Church of San Francisco de Asís (the patron saint of the region), the second-largest cathedral in the Yucatán (the largest is in Mérida). While somewhat run-down, this three-doored basilica still maintains an aura of its past glory.

As you leave Hunucmá to continue on to Celestún, the route passes through two smaller towns, Tetiz and Kinchíl. At the far edge of Kinchíl, 9 miles (14 km) beyond Hunucmá, the highway divides into what initially looks like two dirt paths. The only marking is a small, barely decipherable, hand-painted sign that is nailed to one of the buildings. Whether or not you see the sign, turn right for Celestún.

CELESTÚN From Hunucmá to Celestún, there are 40 miles (64 km) of lonely, flat highway surrounded by jungle. After nearly an hour's drive through this wilderness and almost without warning, a bridge marks the outskirts of Celestún.

Across the bridge, on the right-hand side, is the National Center for the Study of Aquatic Birds. With luck, you may be able to persuade one of the ornithology students from the center to give you a personalized tour (in English) of the marshlands, replete with an academic explanation of the breeding, migration, and nesting habits of each of the 230 species that inhabit the refuge. More likely, you will have to hire a boat and guide at the bridge. A 2½-hour tour will run about $20 to $25, depending on the size of the boat, time of year, and availability of guides (the old supply-and-demand factor comes into play). Make sure to check the boat before agreeing on a price. The best bet is a motorized fiberglass craft with a captain who looks at least old enough to have a learner's permit to drive in the States. This is the place to use insect repellent, since mosquitoes and other pests can be a major problem, particularly during the summer. Also, don't forget sunscreen, rubber-soled shoes, and a hat. Most of the trip is in open marsh, where the sun's intensity is multiplied by the still reflections on the water.

It takes about half an hour to get to the flamingos' feeding grounds. Unlike Río Lagartos, Celestún is not a breeding ground for these rosy-plumed birds, but there is usually a small colony of white fledglings feeding to one side of the adult population. As you approach the birds, your guide will shut off the motor to keep from spooking them. Once they notice human visitors, they will take off running in near military formation, charging across the shallow waters until they gather enough speed to take flight. During the mating season (April through May), there can be as many as 100,000 flamingos at any given site. As they flood the air, the birds create an awe-inspiring giant cloud of pink that sails gracefully overhead.

When you've had your fill of flamingos in flight, ask your guide to take you through the *manglares* (mangrove forests) that surround the marsh. There is a hidden pool with an underground spring, which feeds the marsh with sweet water that is ideal for a quick dip to cool off before taking the boat back to your car. Also to be seen at Celestún are colonies of pelican, loon, stork, crane, avocet, and heron. Sea turtles are common as well, as are spider monkeys and ocelots, but chances are you won't catch a glimpse of these creatures unless you are in the marsh either at dawn or at dusk.

Although none of the restaurants in Celestún could be categorized as premier dining establishments, there are a few open-air cafés downtown (all one street of it), along the ocean shore, which offer fresh seafood at extremely reasonable prices. The best (and cleanest) is the *Celestún* (on Calles 11 and 12). A family-run business, this place specializes in seafood dishes. The *Gutiérrez,* a modest, 18-room hotel down the street, has overhead fans and hot-water showers. The rooms are meager, but clean enough (see *Best en Route*). To return to Mérida, retrace your steps, traveling east along the unmarked road.

DAY TRIP 3: UXMAL

The ruins of Uxmal (pronounced Oosh-*mahl*) are about 50 miles (80 km) southwest of Mérida on the "Puuc Trail." Take the left-hand fork at Umán, which will put you on Route 261, 11 miles (18 km) beyond Mérida; after another 30 miles (48 km), bear right at the fork at Muna. Not as large as Chichén Itzá, Uxmal is equally fascinating. The buildings here are purely Maya in style, without later Toltec influences, and are lavishly decorated with masks, cornices, and mosaics.

UMÁN Only 11 miles (18 km) southwest of Mérida, Umán is a thriving suburb of the Yucatán's capital city. In earlier days, however, Umán was a great city in its own right. The majestic domed early-17th-century Cathedral of San Francisco de Asís, which can be seen from several miles away, is evidence of its past glory. Occupying 2 city blocks, the church constitutes one of the finest examples of Franciscan architecture in all of Mexico.

YAXOCOPOIL HACIENDA Off the main highway at Umán is the "Puuc Trail," so-called for the Pre-Classic- and Classic-style designs of the Maya buildings in this central part of the state. Although not generally as large as later

Maya ruins, the "Puuc" buildings tend to be more delicately decorated. They are particularly famous for their geometric and snake patterns, which are best appreciated from an angle at the front of the buildings.

Just 6 miles (10 km) past Umán is a big sign that says "Yaxocopoil." For those who have the time and want to catch a glimpse of the Yucatán's past, this combination museum, soft-drink stand, and colonial ruins was once one of the largest *henequén* (hemp) plantations in the region. When synthetic fiber brought the age of the great *henequén* barons to an end, the plantation was abandoned and left to decay. A few of the old-timers in the town used to work on the plantation and will spin a few yarns (generously spiced with personal embellishments) about the "good old days." Though much smaller now, the plantation is still in operation, and visitors can watch *henequén* being processed. There is a small museum with photos and relics (open Mondays through Saturdays from 8 AM to 6 PM, Sundays from 9 AM to 1 PM), plus a rather rustic café that offers cold drinks and a view of this once majestic estate.

UXMAL With its towering, rounded pyramid and breathtaking nunnery, Uxmal, the major site of the Maya classic period (AD 600-1000), was one of the sites to which the Maya returned again and again during the course of their civilization. The name means "three times built," but apparently it was actually abandoned and rebuilt as many as five times. Uxmal is generally considered the best example of the fine, classic Maya architecture: The temples and other buildings are beautifully proportioned and designed.

Why Uxmal was abandoned is not as hard to fathom as why it was built in the first place, or why it was rebuilt so many times: It has no water. The Yucatán is one vast limestone slab with rivers running underground. Here and there the rock has caved in, forming cenotes (sinkholes), great natural wells of water. These are prominent at other ruins, but there are none at Uxmal. The Maya carved their own giant reservoirs, but clearly there were years when the rains failed to come. Sculptures of Chac, the elephant-nosed rain god — the most important god in the Maya pantheon — are seen throughout Uxmal.

The two largest pyramids, the Temples of the Dwarf and Magician, contain intricate masks, panels, and mosaics. The Palace of the Governor, a majestic structure 320 feet long and 40 feet wide, is built on multiple levels with vaulted passages and lateral wings containing exquisite lat-ticework and mosaics. It's considered by many to be the most beautiful of all the Maya structures in Central America. Here, some 20,000 hand-cut stones have been set into acres of geometric friezes.

The House of Turtles is a well-proportioned and simply adorned struc-ture northeast of the Governor's Palace. The nunnery is the quadrangle where vestals allegedly spent a licentious final year of worldly pleasure before their sacrifice to appease Chac.

Many of the ruins at Uxmal remain almost unexplored, and there is plenty to see. Archaeologists move slowly among the remote sections of the ruins, sifting through every spoonful of earth as it is removed. This is why Uxmal's large ball courts remain mostly wilderness. The House of the Old Woman and the Temple of the Phalli (a distinctly unerotic structure) still await further exploration. Guided tours through the ruins usually take about 4 hours; many travelers like to take the tour and then wander among the monuments on their own. Devotees of Maya culture usually journey to the ruins at Kabah, only 14 miles (23 km) from Uxmal (see below), but visitors whose interests are more casual tend to be disappointed, since the ruins at Kabah are mostly rubble.

The best way to appreciate Uxmal is after dark, during the sound-and-light show presented nightly except Mondays at 7 PM in Spanish and 9 PM in English. The script is a bit inane — although it does convey something of the feeling of the place — but the lighting is spectacular. Uxmal is noted for the marvelously intricate geometric designs worked into its sculptures (in true "Puuc" fashion). These can be seen and appreciated much better under artificial light than in the blazing sun.

If you are looking for an adventure with exotic appeal, there are several very good hotels adjacent to the abandoned Maya city where you can spend the night gazing at the beauty of this extraordinary place (see *Best en Route*).

KABAH This ceremonial center 14 miles (23 km) south of Uxmal was built in the same architectural style, though smaller. Largely unrestored, Kabah is most notable for its Palace of the Masks, whose façade is covered with innumerable carved masks of the rain god, Chac. Most impressive, too, is Codz-Pop, a rare spiral-shape pyramid. Also found at Kabah is the great arch, the gateway to the ancient causeway linking this city with Uxmal. Open from 8 AM to 5 PM. Closed Mondays. Admission charge.

SAYIL and LABNÁ A paved road has replaced the old dirt lane that leads to these two Maya ceremonial centers, which previously could be reached only by jeep. Sayil is 20 miles (32 km) from Uxmal; Labná, 5 miles (8 km) farther. Little of either site has been restored, but it is still possible to appreciate the fine sculpture and carving that decorate the façades of their palaces. Open 8 AM to 5 PM. Closed Mondays. Admission charge.

Day-trippers should take Route 261 north back to Mérida. However, travelers who are continuing beyond Mérida on this route through the western Yucatán should instead stay on Route 261 south to Campeche, 89 miles (142 km) past Labná (see *En route to Campeche,* below).

En route to Campeche When leaving Mérida to continue the route through the western Yucatán, drive south on Route 261 toward the port city of Campeche. The entire 139-mile (222-km) trip should take about 4 hours. That leaves plenty of time to poke around the various Maya ruins along the route (see *Day Trip 3: Uxmal*) and still get to Campeche by dusk.

BOLONCHÉN DE REJÓN This side trip on the way to Campeche is a must for spelunkers. Even for amateurs, these stalactite-studded caverns 200 feet below the earth near the Campeche state line, about 34 miles (55 km) southwest of Uxmal, are worth a look. Bolonchén, which means "nine wells," refers to the nine Maya cisterns once used to supply water to the inhabitants in pre-Columbian times. The de Rejón part of the name comes from Manuel De Rejón, a local hero who drafted the Mexican constitutional amendment that guarantees the right of habeas corpus for all prisoners.

For a small fee, a guide will escort you through the subterranean passages. Don't try to explore these caves on your own. They go on for miles with extremely dangerous reaches, and at present, only the first few chambers have been fitted with lights and handrails.

When you leave Bolonchén de Rejón, you will be entering the state of Campeche (pronounced Com-*pay*-chay), home to over half of Mexico's shrimp boats. The word "campeche" is actually a Maya acronym for "land of serpents and ticks," but don't let the name throw you. Rich with oil, Campeche is a place where the pace is slow and the living is easy. In fact, if a Mexican wants to say that a person is lazy or tends to put things off, he will call him a *campechano*. A meal, for example, can take up to 3 or even 4 hours in Campeche, where the idea of rushing through anything, especially something as enjoyable as savoring good food in the company of friends and family, is as alien as snow in the tropics. Foreigners, used to the hurried world of fast-food restaurants and a 45-minute lunch break, sometimes find the leisurely tempo of *campechano* service hard to adjust to; smart visitors will just lean back and enjoy the laissez-faire lifestyle.

HOPELCHÉN About 21 miles (34 km) south of Bolonchén de Rejón, the road angles sharply to the right at Hopelchén. Founded in 1622, this town's only distinction is that it was once totally surrounded by a military fort constructed on top of Maya ruins during the latter half of the last century. Most of the fort walls have since collapsed, but remnants of the structure, intermingled with hints of small pyramids, can still be discerned by a careful observer. There is also a 17th-century church, dedicated to St. Anthony, with a giant wooden altar composed of ten hand-painted portraits of the patron.

Campeche is 56 miles (90 km) west of Hopelchén on Route 261.

CAMPECHE One of Mexico's least-visited and most picturesque port towns, Campeche has been walled and fortressed from the early days of the Spanish conquest. No one has ever bothered to promote tourism here, but with a couple of fine hotels and some unique monuments, Campeche is waiting to be discovered. Its fortresses and walls resemble a Caribbean city, unique along Mexico's Gulf Coast.

Cortés first landed on Mexican soil at the site of Campeche in 1517; founded in 1540, the city steadily increased in importance. The conquistadores discovered logwood, a rare and costly source of dye, growing in the nearby forests. By the mid-1550s, they were getting rich exporting the precious commodity to Europe. Though remote and isolated, Campeche rapidly grew into one of the most thriving cities of New Spain — and attracted the attention of Caribbean buccaneers. Rich as Campeche was, it was also defenseless. The city was first sacked by William Parck and his band of cutthroats in 1597. Thirty-five years later, in 1632, a pirate known as Diego el Mulato did it again. Then came Peg Leg (yes, there really was a swashbuckler by that name) and Laurent de Graff, a Dutch adventurer whom the locals dubbed Lorencillo. L'Olonois of France, who had a sweetheart in town, was another frequent visitor. This Frenchman earned a reputation as the most sadistic of buccaneers, due to his habit of eating his victim's eyeballs! In 1685, when Lewis Scott, another buccaneer, sacked the place once again, the city decided to protect itself. The people began work on the wall and forts in 1686, a task that took 18 years to complete. Parts of the wall have since been removed, evidence of more peaceful times, but the two main gates and seven of the original eight fortresses remain. The wall and the gates now offer endless possibilities to photographers and watercolorists, who may well never want to leave.

The former Fort of San Pedro is now a handicrafts market. The tourist office (in the former Fort of Santa Rosa; phone: 981-67364) is where you can get a guide to show you around town. The rooftop of San Pedro is much as it was in days of old, its fighting deck heavy with now-ancient cannon. How these quaint guns managed to stop marauding men-of-war from taking everything in sight is not easy to understand, but clearly they did. The marksmen must have been remarkable. With a bit of persuasion and a few extra pesos, your guide will take you to the secret passageways beneath the fort. Now mostly sealed off with bricks, these tunnels once linked many houses in the city. Some of the passages were built during the Maya period and were simply expanded by the Spanish. These underground hiding places sheltered women and children when pirate ships came into view.

The *Casa del Teniente del Rey* (Lieutenant del Rey House) has been converted into the *Campeche Regional Museum,* with an interesting collection of Maya objects, including a jade mask and a collection of jewelry discovered in the Colakmul tomb. Across from the main square and City Hall on the *malecón* (closed Mondays; admission charge). *San Miguel,* the handsomest of all Campeche's fortresses, is now a museum displaying pirate arms and portraits of the worst scoundrels who harried the city. There is also a model of walled Campeche as it looked nearly 3 centuries ago. The guides are quite fond of telling horror stories about how San Miguel's moat was filled with quicklime instead of water, or how the water was stocked with crocodiles. They are somewhat vague about whether any malefactor ever earned his grisly reward by being tumbled into the moat. Open daily. Admission charge. Calle 59.

Church lovers, who will find pickings pretty slim along the Yucatán Peninsula, can score comparatively heavily in Campeche. The cathedral on the main plaza was completed in 1546 — only 6 years after Don Francisco de Montejo y León ordered construction to begin, on the same day that he founded the city. The San Francisco Monastery, just off the *malecón* (seafront esplanade), is nearly as old. Mass was first said here in 1546. About 20 years later, the grandson of Hernán Cortés was baptized here at a font still in use today.

Campeche has its modern side, too. The brightly colored Government Palace has been dubbed "the jukebox" by irreverent local citizens, and the modern Legislative Palace is known as "the flying saucer." In fact, these modern structures were rather carefully designed to fit in with Campeche's unique native architecture and have completely avoided the glass-box look so prevalent in many high-rise sections of Mexican cities. Nonetheless they have offended the taste of the city's proud and conservative older guard. Other modern additions that have pleased residents more are the city's growing network of wide, handsome boulevards and the futuristic University City — rivaled only by the suburb of the same name in Mexico City.

Campeche is noted for its seafood, especially the shrimp it sells all over the world. Some crab (*cangrejo moro*), pompano, and a black snapper (known as *esmedregal*) are local favorites. Campeche is also known for its intriguing seafood combinations. In addition to shrimp and oyster cocktails, there are *campechanos,* in which both are served together. Light beer and dark beer are served half-and-half, too, on request. The restaurant in the *Baluartes* hotel, Campeche's most modern hostelry (see *Best en Route*), serves good seafood and accepts major credit cards. The *Miramar* restaurant, across the street from the Government Palace, is less expensive and more crowded, but serves food that's at least as good as the *Baluartes*'s, in a junky waterfront setting.

EDZNÁ Archaeology buffs will want to make a side trip to this exceptional Maya site — a shining example of classic Maya architecture. Only 38 miles (61 km) southeast of Campeche, Edzná is surprisingly easy to reach. Follow Route 180 southeast to a town called Cayal, 26 miles (42 km) from Campeche. Turn right and follow a rather bumpy Route 188 for 12 miles (19 km) and you will almost literally run right into this site.

One of the oldest ruins in the Yucatán, Edzná is believed to have been inhabited as early as 600 BC. The name, which translates to "House of the Grimaces," refers to the two grim masks that are encrusted in the base of the Five-Story Temple, the largest construction in the ancient city. Because of the "Puuc" architecture, characterized by elaborately decorated façades, pre-Columbian authorities have linked the builders of this 3-square-mile vestige with the classic Maya who populated Guatemala.

While the pyramids themselves are not particularly impressive (only three of the structures have been restored), Edzná boasts the most advanced hydraulic system in the whole of the Maya world. Because of its geographic location, the area receives little or no rain except during the summer. Consequently, the resourceful engineers who laid out the city designed a complex network of dammed reservoirs and irrigation canals to store and distribute water.

Towering 120 feet high, the Five-Story Temple is clearly the center of attraction in Edzná. The steps are overgrown with weeds and in poor repair, so it's not a very good idea to plan on scaling this edifice. However, in order to get an overview of the main plaza below and the rest of the ruins, you probably can work your way up the temple's first or second story without any major calamities. To the left is a smaller pyramid, Paal U'Na, or the House of the Moon. Just behind this building is a small acropolis, which can barely be distinguished in the underbrush. Opposite Paal U'Na is the Northern Platform, with five chambers that apparently were used for storage of sacred treasures. There is also a ball court and elongated annex that must have served as a living quarters for Edzná's chieftains and shamans, who are buried beneath heavy foliage.

En route from Campeche Unlike the winding Ruta Puuc, which snakes its way from ruin to ruin, the western road back to Mérida is a straight, smooth shot from Campeche. Route 261 east of the city picks up Route 180 north in Chenocoyi, a tiny village (if a few thatch huts can be called a village) 17 miles (27 km) out of town. From then on, the road heads in only one direction, so it is practically impossible to get lost. Because the road is well paved and adequately maintained, the 121-mile (194-km) drive will take only about 2 hours. The main stop along the way will undoubtedly be Oxkintók. Constructed sometime during the 5th century, this site was excavated during the late 1980s by European archaeologists, through funding provided by the Spanish Ministry of Culture as part of a program to commemorate the 500th anniversary in 1992 of the discovery of the Americas. It is believed to have been the largest Maya city in the Yucatán Peninsula. You may also want to stop off in Becal to pick up a Panama hat.

POMÚCH Located 23 miles (37 km) northeast of Campeche on Route 180, Pomúch is renowned throughout the region for its spongy, sweet bread, purported to be the best in Mexico. As you drive past, you will see a series of roadside stands selling this sugary fare. As long as the bread is sealed in plastic bags, you might want to sample it and find out firsthand why the town has gained such acclaim.

BECAL If you want to buy a Panama hat, Becal, 32 miles (51 km) farther north on Route 180, is the best place in Mexico to find one. Using only the finest straw from the *jipijapa* palm, the inhabitants of this town have been mass-producing these hats for over a century and exporting them to literally every corner of the globe. As you drive by, you may notice that most

151

of the houses in Becal have large mounds in their courtyards that resemble oversize firing kilns for ceramics. These are in fact manmade caverns which are used to keep the straw moist and flexible during the weaving process. In addition to hats, the Becalans are very adept at fashioning shoes, handbags, necklaces, and other items from the *jipijapa* palm.

OXKINTÓK Past the Campeche-Yucatán state border, 11 miles (18 km) north of Becal, is the modern-day town of Oxkintók. Turn right on the dirt path marked "Maxcanu" and continue about 4 miles (6 km) to find the archaeological ruins. Don't expect to find a lot of signs indicating how to get to this site. It was virtually unknown until 1986, and has been open to the public only since 1991.

Excavated courtesy of a grant from the Spanish government, Oxkintók, constructed in the 5th century, is now considered to be the largest Maya vestige on the peninsula. Although archaeologists are still trying to determine its exact size, experts estimate that the city extended over at least 7 square miles, and during its heyday, in the late 9th century, Oxkintók probably was inhabited by as many as 50,000 Maya. Oxkintók, which means "Three Stone Suns," was in fact the New York City of the Maya world, serving as a merchandising and distribution center for the entire region, as well as a gateway for trade with the Mexican mainland.

The main building, Santunsát, is a giant 3-story labyrinth, the only one of its kind in the Yucatán; it's so massive it can take days to explore. This rectangular edifice measures over 20 feet high and includes seven long passageways on the ground floor that intertwine in a complex maze to eventually reach the second floor, which has eight meandering chambers. The third and final level has only four tangled hallways to surmount, leading to a narrow exit on the east side. To date, no one has been able to determine with certainty what function this structure served. The local townsfolk maintain that those who offended the gods were locked in its chambers as punishment for their crimes and could find their way out again only if they repented. Modern scholars, on the other hand, contend that the maze has a more esoteric significance, suggesting that the building's 3 stories represent the 3 levels of the universe — the underworld, the earth, and the heavens. Other theories about Santunsát include that it might have been an observatory or a burial site, a premise supported by the fact that a tomb and small burial urn were discovered nearby during the latest excavations. A word to the wise: Do not attempt to explore this labyrinth without an experienced guide, or you could spend the rest of your vacation trying to solve the mystery of Santunsát from the inside out.

There are also several other less impressive, if less intimidating, structures at Oxkintók. Among these are a mammoth-size ball court, 27 stelae etched with Maya glyphs, two rather ho-hum pyramids, and a huge Olmec-like stone head of the sun god Kinich Ahua, which suggests a cultural link between the two civilizations.

Exploring this site can take up to 4 hours (or longer — *much* longer — if you get lost in the labyrinth), so amateur archaeologists who want more than a superficial glance should give themselves plenty of time to enjoy it by leaving Campeche early in the morning.

Alternate route from Campeche If you want to continue the Yucatán Loop, drive southeast to Chetumal, stopping to take in the ruins of Kohunlich, but this is not a journey for the timid-spirited. The trip is 282 miles (451 km), but it is a tedious odyssey that can take up to 7 hours to complete because every few miles the roads are pitted with industrial strength *topes* (road bumps), which can wreak havoc on both your timetable and your shock absorbers. This is wild jungle country, and traveling these parts is similar to roaming around the headwaters of the Amazon. Roads are new in this part of Mexico, and amenities are sparse. It is a good idea to take along a box lunch and fill up whenever a gas station comes into view.

From Campeche, follow Route 180 south for 41 miles (66 km) to Champotón, the last stop on the Gulf of Mexico coast. Champotón is noteworthy because it was here in 1517 that Francisco Hernández de Córdoba and his party celebrated the first mass on the American continent. Route 261 leaves Route 180 at Champotón and continues due south to Escárcega. Little more than a collection of huts, Escárcega is where you pick up Route 186 east to Chetumal. From here on, the jungles close in. It is not unusual to see an ocelot or tapir darting across the road. Tarantulas on the asphalt are downright common. The scenery is not particularly beautiful, but neither is it quickly forgotten.

Underscoring the remoteness of the region is the customs shed at the Quintana Roo state line. No one driving in has to stop, but vehicles leaving Quintana Roo are required to submit to a customs inspection at the checkpoint. As a free zone, beyond the reach of Mexico's protective tariffs, Quintana Roo has always been a base for smugglers and gun-runners. A word of warning: If you choose to take this less beaten path, do so with care. The area is notorious for *bandidos* (highway bandits) who prey on unsuspecting motorists by placing sharp rocks in the middle of the road to cause mechanical breakdowns. Should you have a sudden blowout along the way, do not stop immediately. Instead, slow down slightly and continue at least half a mile or so down the highway before pulling over. This will no doubt damage the tire beyond repair, but it could well protect you from the hands of a modern-day pirate. For detailed information on Chetumal and alternate routes back to Cancún, see *The Yucatán Peninsula: Cancún to Chetumal* in this section.

BEST EN ROUTE

CHECKING IN This area offers a wide assortment of hotels, some elegant, some downright primitive. With the exception of Mérida, many villages and towns in the Yucatán are simply too small and too informally arranged to require street addresses for hotels and restaurants. Most towns have only one or two streets. Therefore, occasionally a specific address (as we know it) may not exist. For a double room, expect to pay $155 or more at a very expensive hotel; $90 to $150 at expensive places; $40 to $80 in moderate places; and $35 or under in inexpensive ones.

VALLADOLID

María de la Luz Pleasantly modern, it's a nice little provincial hotel with a swimming pool, restaurant, and bar with live entertainment. 195 Calle 42 (phone: 985-62071). Moderate.

Mesón del Marquéz Heavy on atmosphere, this old-fashioned colonial inn is one of a dying breed, with 24 rooms and 2 suites, a restaurant-bar, and gardens. 203 Calle 39 (phone: 985-62073; fax: 985-62280). Moderate.

RÍO LAGARTOS

Nefertití With a nice view of the lagoon, this modest place is clean and comfortable enough, although amenities are sparse. There is a restaurant (which closes early), and overhead fans, but *no* hot water or air conditioning. Still, given that the 20-room inn is the only hotel in town with anything even approaching a two-star rating, you haven't got a lot of options. No credit cards accepted. 123 Calle 14 (phone: 987-32668 in Río Lagartos, then ask for 14154). Inexpensive.

CHICHÉN ITZÁ

Mayaland Overlooking the ruins, this luxury resort has 65 large, old-fashioned rooms including 12 villas, a restaurant, cocktail terrace, swimming pool, and evening entertainment. Carr. 180 (phone: 99-252133 or 99-252122 in Mérida; 800-235-4079 in the US; fax: 99-252397). Expensive.

Dolores Alba Absolutely lovely and a nice change of pace from hotel stays, this country house has only 18 rooms, each with a private terrace. There's also a cozy dining room, pool, and tropical grounds. Km 122, between Chichén Itzá and the Balankanchén Caves (phone: 99-213745 in Mérida; fax: 99-283163 in Mérida). Moderate.

Hacienda Chichén Just a century ago this was a private hacienda; today it is a hotel with rooms available in individual bungalows. Facilities include ceiling fans, restaurant, bar, and a pool. Open from November through *Easter*. Chichén Itzá (phone: 985-62462; 99-248892 in Mérida; 800-223-4084 in the US; fax: 99-245011 in Mérida). Moderate.

Misión Park Inn Chichén Itzá This modern hotel has 50 air conditioned rooms, bar, restaurant, pool, and lovely grounds. Pisté, about a mile (1.6 km) from Chichén Itzá (phone: 99-56271 in Mérida; 91-800-90038 toll-free within Mexico; or 800-437-PARK in the US; fax: 99-237665 in Mérida). Moderate.

Villa Arqueológica One of the archaeological "inns" run by Club Med, only 5 minutes from the ruins. All 44 rooms are air conditioned, and there is a pool, tennis, and a good French restaurant (phone: 985-62830; 5-203-3086 in Mexico City; 800-CLUB-MED in the US; fax: 5-203-0681 in Mexico City). Moderate.

Pirámide Inn So comfortable, it's hard to leave it to explore the ruins. Facilities include a pool, tennis courts, lush gardens, restaurant, bar, even a book exchange. The 47 air conditioned rooms are adequate. Pisté (phone: 99-252122, ext. 151; 800-262-9296 in the US). Inexpensive.

MÉRIDA

Los Aluxes A modern 109-room hostelry, it rises white and impressively spotless between Paseo de Montejo and the zocalo. It has an outdoor pool and poolside bars, a dining room, and a cheerful coffee shop whose placemats are the best city map available. 444 Calle 60, between Calles 49 and 51 (phone: 99-242199; 800-782-8395 in the US; fax: 99-233858). Expensive.

D'Champs Though the interior of this 88-room property was totally renovated, its stately colonial façade was left intact. There are 2 restaurants, a swimming pool, and a score of small boutiques. 543 Calle 70 (phone: 99-248655; 800-448-8687 in the US; fax: 99-236024). Expensive.

Holiday Inn Built in the colonial manner, on the foundation of one of the old *henequén* (hemp) plantations, this place has 213 rooms and suites, a tennis court, pool, nightclub, and a restaurant. Air conditioned. Just off Paseo Montejo at Av. Colón and Calle 60 (phone: 99-256877; 800-HOLIDAY in the US; fax: 99-257755). Expensive.

Residencial This flamingo-toned, 6-story mansion looks as if it was taken from the set of *Gone with the Wind*. The 66 spacious rooms have color TV sets and air conditioning; there's also an elegant dining room and a large pool. 589 Calle 59 at Calle 76 (phone: 99-243099 or 99-244844; 800-826-6842 in the US; fax: 99-212230). Expensive.

Calinda Panamericana Mérida A Quality Inns International property with a lobby and reception area housed in a turn-of-the-century mansion, it has 110 modern, air conditioned rooms, color TV sets, a restaurant, and a bar. There is a Mexican fiesta Friday and Saturday nights; regional dances from the state of Yucatán are performed other nights. Downtown at 455 Calle 59 (phone: 99-239111; 800-782-8395 in the US; fax: 99-248090). Moderate.

El Castellaño With 170 rooms, it's one of Mérida's largest and sleekest hotels (it's air conditioned), including a spacious, hacienda-style lobby. Amenities include shops, restaurant, bar, and swimming pool. 513 Calle 57, between Calles 62 and 64 (phone: 99-230100; 800-424-8100 in the US; fax: 99-230110). Moderate.

Del Gobernador Tidy and tasteful, this 61-room spot offers a good restaurant, live music several times a week, and a very small pool. 535 Calle 59 at Calle 66 (phone: 99-237133; 800-223-4084 in the US; fax: 99-281590). Moderate.

María del Carmen The modern-looking, white mortar and glass exterior of this Best Western property belies its charmingly colonial interior design. Amenities include a gardened courtyard and a superb dining room, as well as a bar and a gift shop. Each of the 100 rooms has air conditioning and a color TV set. 550 Calle 63 between Calles 68 and 70 (phone: 99-239133; 800-528-1234 in the US; fax 99-239290). Moderate.

Mérida Misión Park Inn Entrance is through a beautiful 19th-century mansion. The 147 rooms are located in a modern tower, and have air conditioning and cable TV. There's a coffee shop, lobby bar, and restaurant. Three blocks from the zocalo at 491 Calle 60 (phone: 99-239500; 800-437-PARK in the US; fax: 99-237665). Moderate.

Gran This replica of a turn-of-the-century French hotel has elaborate ceilings, columns, and large, old-fashioned rooms, some air conditioned. The 5-story building centers around a delightful patio. There is a good dining room. Cepeda Peraza Park (phone: 99-247730; fax: 99-247622). Inexpensive.

Montejo Palace Quiet, with 90 air conditioned rooms, some with small balconies. In addition to a dining room and a good coffee shop, *Las Farolas,* there is a cocktail lounge and a pool. 483-C Paseo Montejo (phone: 99-247644; 800-221-6509 in the US; fax: 99-280388). Inexpensive.

Paseo de Montejo A 5-story modern colonial-style establishment, it has 92 air conditioned rooms, color TV sets, restaurant, bar, and pool. 482 Paseo de Montejo (phone: 99-239033; fax: 99-280388). Inexpensive.

NOTE   For our choices of restaurants in Mérida, see *Eating Out,* below.

PROGRESO

Paraíso Maya Set on a wide strip of beach at Progreso, this colonial-style hostelry was built to resemble a small Mexican village. There are restaurants, bars, a pool, and disco. The rate includes meals, drinks, and water sports. Km 32 Carr. Progreso-Telchac (phone: 993-281351; 800-223-4084 in the US; fax: 993-232700). Very expensive.

Fiesta Inn The finest in town, this 38-room hostelry opened in late 1990 to accommodate the sudden flood of businesspeople and government officials cashing in on the rebirth of the city's port facilities. It has a lobby bar, restaurant, cafeteria, swimming pool, and gift shop. All rooms are air conditioned and have cable TV. On the *malecón* (phone: 993-50300). Expensive.

Sian-Ka'an This 9-suite, air conditioned inn is a holdover from earlier days when service was personalized and mass anything was unthinkable. Owner Edgardo Sánchez attends to each guest's needs on a one-on-one basis and the home-style menu changes daily. Definitely a class act. Calle 17 on the Chelem Highway at Yucalpetén (phone: 993-54017; 99-282582 or 99-215358 in Mérida). Moderate.

Tropical Suites Another small establishment, this 10-unit place is geared to families and groups that prefer to rough it and do for themselves. Kitchenettes, overhead fans, and big balconies with a view of the ocean. *Malecón* at Calle 70 (phone: 993-51263). Moderate.

Posada Juan Carlos Owned by a Swiss family, this 16-room hotel operates primarily for European tour groups. The rooms are clean, but stripped down to the minimum and devoid of any personal touches. 148 Calle 74 (phone: 993-51076). Inexpensive.

Real del Mar A 10-unit spot with overhead fans, a restaurant-bar, and a big sandy beach all to itself. Calles 19 and 20 (no phone). Inexpensive.

CELESTÚN

Gutiérrez The only halfway presentable place in town, this 18-unit facility is a bit reminiscent of a dormitory for seminary students — not much to offer but a cot, hot shower, and overhead fans. 107 Calle 12 (phone: 99-246348 in Mérida). Inexpensive.

UXMAL

Hacienda Uxmal Elegant and charming, it has 80 large, cool rooms, some air conditioned, that overlook lovely gardens. Restaurant, bar, shops, and 2 pools (phone: 99-252133 or 99-252122 in Mérida; 800-235-4079 in the US; fax: 99-252397 in Mérida). Expensive.

Misión Park Inn Uxmal A modern, air conditioned place, with 50 rooms, a restaurant, and pool (phone/fax: 99-247308 in Mérida; 800-437-PARK in the US). Moderate.

Villa Arqueológica Right in front of the ruins, this 49-unit air conditioned hostelry is equipped with the standard facilities of all Club Med Villas Arqueológicas: a good French restaurant, pool, and tennis (phone: 99-247053 in Mérida; 5-203-3086 in Mexico City; 800-CLUB-MED in the US; fax: 5-203-0681 in Mexico City). Moderate.

Alhambra Its 100 rooms are air conditioned, and there is a restaurant, coffee shop, disco, pool, and satellite TV. 85 Av. Resurgimiento (phone: 981-66822 or 981-66323; fax: 981-66132). Expensive.

Ramada Inn This is a fine hotel with 119 rooms, a swimming pool, bar, disco, and restaurant. 51 Av. Ruíz Cortinez (phone: 981-62233; 800-228-3838 in the US; fax: 981-11618). Expensive.

Baluartes Here is a handsome, well-located, traditional hotel that is near the sea, with 102 rooms, a swimming pool and restaurant. 61 Av. Ruíz Cortinez (phone: 981-63911; fax: 981-65765). Moderate.

López Small and friendly, it is known for its charming bar and restaurant. The air conditioned rooms are furnished quite comfortably. 189 Calle 12 (phone: 981-63021). Moderate.

Si-Ho Playa If you want to stay around for more than 1 night, this small 78-unit resort is perfect. With a tennis court, boat rental (about 3 miles/5 km from the hotel), swimming pool, and restaurant, the environment is very relaxing. At Km 35 on the Carr. Campeche–Champotón (phone: 981-64044; fax: 981-66154). Moderate.

EATING OUT IN MÉRIDA The Yucatán has a distinct cuisine, and Mérida's restaurants offer ample culinary opportunities. Very little chili is used in cooking, although it is served alongside the main dish as a sauce. Many meat and fish dishes are wrapped in banana leaves and then baked in outdoor ovens, a method that originated because of the hot climate. Pickled and charcoal-broiled meats are Yucatecan specialties, too. Try the *cochinita pibil* (pork baked in banana leaves); *papadzul* (hard-boiled eggs chopped into a filling for a tortilla, topped with a sauce of ground pumpkin seeds); *panuchos* (open-faced tortilla topped with chicken and pickled onion); and *pollo pibil* (chicken baked with achiote sauce in banana leaves). Expect to pay up to $40 for a meal for two in the restaurants we've listed as expensive; $25 at those places listed as moderate; and about $15 at inexpensive ones. Prices do not include drinks, wine, or tip. Reservations are advised at midday for all expensive places. In the evening, reservations are unnecessary unless otherwise noted. Most restaurants listed below accept MasterCard and Visa; some also accept American Express and Diners Club. Unless otherwise noted, all restaurants are open daily.

Alberto's Continental Patio Set in a lovely colonial mansion with outdoor and indoor dining areas; the Lebanese dishes here are first-rate. There are also some continental and local specialties. The service is very friendly. 482 Calle 64 (phone: 99-285367 or 99-286336). Expensive.

La Casona Fifteen tiled tables with caned chairs rim an interior courtyard with a lovely fountain; there's also an inside dining room, sporting unusual antique barber's chairs at the bar. Italian food, including homemade pasta, is the highlight, but the steaks and seafood rate, too. The restaurant's cellar stocks French and Mexican wines. Open for lunch and dinner. 434 Calle 60 at Calle 47 (phone: 99-238348). Expensive.

Château Valentín Converted from one of Mérida's elegant 18th-century homes, this establishment serves well-prepared regional dishes such as *pollo pibil* as well as international fare. 499-D Calle 58-A at Paseo de Montejo (phone: 99-255690). Expensive.

Le Gourmet Once an elegant home, it specializes in French and creole cooking and is where the local gentry go to celebrate on big nights out. 109-A Av. Pérez Ponce (phone: 99-271970). Expensive.

Pancho's In spite of its Mexican name, the owner is Canadian and the menu is continental, with lots of flambéed dishes prepared tableside. With its ancient photos and Victrola, it resembles an old antiques store — kind of like *Carlos 'n' Charlie's,* Maya-style. Live music and dancing are featured Wednesdays through Saturdays. Dinner only. 509 Calle 59, between Calles 60 and 62 (phone: 99-230942). Expensive.

Picadilly's An elegant English-style pub, but the atmosphere is casual (ties and jackets are not required) and the fine food is strictly gringo: barbecued ribs, onion rings, pasta, and grilled beef, with cherry cheesecake for dessert. Live music and dancing are featured Friday and Saturday evenings. 118 Av. Pérez Ponce (phone: 99-265391). Expensive.

Yannig Named after its inspired chef, this sophisticated spot set in a beautiful old home delivers well-prepared and appetizingly presented dishes, among them crêpes with a mild roquefort sauce, New Orleans–style chicken, and *kermor* (fish and mushrooms in a pastry shell). Open for lunch and dinner; closed Mondays. 105 Av. Pérez Ponce (phone: 99-270339). Expensive.

Los Almendros This is one of the best places to sample the finest in *cochinita pibil, panuchos, pollo pibil,* and other Yucatecan delicacies. Service is slow, so be prepared to spend a long time. 493 Calle 50-A, between Calles 57 and 59, in front of the Plaza de Mejorada (phone: 99-285459). Moderate.

La Cabaña del Tío Tom Borrowing from the American South (*Uncle Tom's Cabin*), this eatery has the best steaks in town — the beef is brought in fresh from Monterrey. The decor is Swiss chalet–style, with an odd little Cuban witchcraft altar to greet visitors at the door. 484 Calle 60, next to *El Tucho* (phone: 99-242289). Moderate.

El Pórtico del Peregrino It consists of romantic courtyards and dining rooms in a chapel-like setting. The low-key atmosphere is enhanced by a menu that includes shrimp grilled in garlic, chicken liver shish kebab, baked eggplant casserole with chicken; also delicious desserts and homemade sangria. On Calle 57 between Calles 60 and 62 (phone: 99-216844). Moderate.

La Prosperidad The local favorite, hands down, it serves Yucatecan dishes in a large, thatch-roofed dining room. A variety of appetizers accompanies each meal. Entertainment is live and lively, as is the ambience. Good fun. Calle 56, corner of Calle 53 (phone: 99-211898). Moderate.

El Tucho Far from fancy, this rustic, *palapas*-roofed restaurant serves some of the finest Yucatecan dishes in town, as well as several Cuban specialties (the chef is from Havana). There is live entertainment day and night; occasionally, it takes on a cabaret atmosphere, but mostly it is Cuban calypso music or a Yucatán folk dance group. 482 Calle 60, between 55 and 57 (phone: 99-242323). Moderate.

El Faisán y El Venado Night owls will like this rustic Yucatecan eatery because it is open daily from 7 AM until 3 AM. Now in its 5th decade, this place has become somewhat of a tradition in Mérida. The decor includes a giant (albeit crude) replica of the main pyramid at Chichén Itzá, cement Maya figures, and glyphs along the cracked walls. There is also live organ music all day and night and some of the best Yucatecan food in the city. 615 Calle 56 at Calle 82 (phone: 99-218352). Inexpensive.

Index